Practical Strategies
for elementary school
INCLUSION

june stride

IEP
RESOURCES

**Practical Strategies for
Elementary School Inclusion**

by June Stride
Edited by Tom Kinney and Elizabeth Ragsdale
Graphic design by Elizabeth Ragsdale
Cartoon creation by Wolfpack Multimedia

An Attainment Publication
©2005 Attainment Company, Inc. All Rights Reserved.
Printed in the United States of America.
ISBN: 1-57861-557-7

RESOURCES

P.O. Box 930160
Verona, Wisconsin 53593-0160
Phone: 1-800-327-4269
Fax: 1-800-942-3865
www.AttainmentCompany.com

Contents

Supplemental Materials

About the Author

Dear Reader and Fellow Educator,

One of the first things an enthusiastic new teacher discovers is that becoming a "professional" is no easy matter; it's a journey over bumpy roads with potholes and detours at unanticipated locations. I have found it's often these unexpected (and at the time, unwanted) diversions that have forced me to stretch and grow. I suppose, looking back over my educational career, that I should say I was fortunate in having had so many growth opportunities!

It is those same bumps, potholes and growth opportunities that have led me to write this book. As author, parent, teacher, administrator, spokesperson and public speaker, I have had a wealth of educational learning experiences. My professional background encompasses work with students K through post high school ages, of exceptional abilities and disabilities, in the public and the private sector, as well as in a maximum-security prison for youthful offenders. Consequently, throughout the years, my peers and my students have patiently taught me about change, about options and, of course, about opportunities. Thanks to them I can share firsthand from my perspective and efforts in a variety of roles.

I am a true believer in the "power of one" and hope that you may use your distinctive talents to contribute to the empowerment of all your students. May this book speed you on your journey.

Respectfully,
June Stride, Ed.D.

Honors and Awards

Who's Who in American Education
Who's Who in the World
Who's Who of American Women
Who's Who
Honorary Life Member of New York State
    Congress of Parents and Teachers
Recipient of the Healthy Living Award for
    the Images book series, one of the top ten
    educational publications

Publications

Co-author: Images Human Sexuality series:
    Changes, Choices, and Challenges
Co-author: *Street Smarts: A Substance Abuse*
    Prevention Program
Author: *Practical Strategies for Including High*
    School Students with Behavioral Disabilities

Acknowledgments

I am especially grateful for the blessings of three special men in my life: First, my dad who encouraged me to write about my experiences in hopes that others might benefit; second, my dearest friend and professional collaborator, Rick Wolfsdorf, who has inspired and critiqued each word; and third, my beloved husband, Bill Stride, who gave me the time, kept me on focus and read and polished each page

1

What Is Inclusion?

AN UNEXPECTED CHALLENGE

Teresa was puzzled by her mixed feelings and unease about beginning a new career as an elementary school teacher. She had weighed carefully the pros and cons of giving up her lucrative, but highly frustrating, job in the business world to become a teacher. She thought she had resolved all the issues. She loved children and wanted her efforts to make a difference. She said to herself that perhaps her current anxiety was just normal new job jitters. But as she replayed the recent conversation with Mr. Roberts, her new boss and principal of Pine Street Elementary, she thought not.

It had happened yesterday when Mr. Roberts and Teresa were sharing a quiet pre-school "get to know each other" conversation in his office, discussing teaching procedures and her responsibilities. After a tour of the school, including a peek into her classroom, he had suggested that she might feel more comfortable if they reviewed her class roster of 24 fourth graders. Teresa readily agreed.

Teresa asked: "Can you give me any helpful insights? As you can imagine, I am anxious to begin preparing myself mentally for Monday."

Mr. Roberts ran his finger down the list, stopping to comment on each name. "George is a charmer, bright, helpful and considerate. Tomas is a small, shy boy, a loner who so far has rarely contributed in class. Angelique has been a handful, but considering the number of foster homes she has been passed through, it's hardly surprising."

Continuing on, Mr. Roberts demonstrated his familiarity with his student body: "And these last four children are classified as students with special needs and will require your closest attention. I know you completed the necessary special education courses to get your certification, so you are familiar with IDEA, IEPs, BIPs and inclusion. You pretty much know what to expect in an inclusion class such as yours."

"Do teachers actually get assigned to inclusion classes without any preparation or forewarning?"

Teresa smiled but said nothing, feeling a cold clamp of terror grip her. She knew the cause; it was the "I" word. She had not been informed that she would be involved in inclusion. She realized it was her ignorance causing the fear and cared not that philosophers proclaimed that the first sign of wisdom is acknowledging ignorance. She wondered what she had gotten herself into and how she would meet this new challenge.

Is it possible that teachers, principals and school districts are still unprepared for inclusion? Do teachers actually get assigned to inclusion classes without any preparation or forewarning? Can it be possible that teachers such as Teresa are quite terror stricken with the prospect of teaching in an inclusion setting? After all, how hard can it be to teach elementary school children, even special needs children? Any dummy can do it, right? And look at all the perks: Health insurance, short days, long vacations, all holidays and the whole summer off!

bottom line

■ ■ ■ ■ ■ ■ ■ ■ ■ ■

Let inclusion be an opportunity for, not an obstacle to, better teaching.

Sure, you know the drill. People hear you are an elementary school teacher and think you barely have to work to collect a paycheck. Their envy becomes painfully obvious as they remark about how nice it is for you to have such an easy job.

The truth is that most teachers entered the teaching profession for the same reason Teresa did, to make a difference by helping children learn. Foremost in their minds was not the typical motivators of money and status but rather the satisfaction of knowing their efforts really mattered to a child's life, to a family and to a society. Also true, many elementary teachers had no idea how all-consuming their responsibilities would be, especially with today's challenges: trauma caused by split families, children increasingly left to their own devices by working parents, children from many cultures and linguistic backgrounds, new federal and state mandates, demands to attain higher standards, web and media reports of class progress and, lastly, inclusion.

This final challenge—inclusion—is the focus of this book. I hope my experiences, my challenges, my opportunities and, yes, my failures will assist you with your teaching efforts in the inclusion classroom.

> *"School districts must make every effort to provide services that allow students with special needs to be educated in the general education environment."*

The "I" word

What is inclusion?

Simply put, educational inclusion means including all children to "the maximum extent appropriate" in the "least restrictive environment" with their nondisabled peers. Inclusion is the opposite of excluding children with special needs to educate them separately. In practical terms, it means that school districts must make every effort to provide whatever services and supports are necessary to allow students with special needs to be educated in the general education environment with their peers. Sometimes inclusion efforts are referred to as "mainstreaming" because the child with special needs enters the general population for education. Sometimes inclusion efforts are also referred to as the Regular Education Initiative (REI) or the General Education Initiative.

What are the legal aspects of inclusion?

Currently, federal law states that *all* children are entitled to a free and appropriate public education. No, this has not always been the case. In fact, this is a fairly recent American legal mandate, in effect only since 1975 (and one considered

bottom line
∎ ∎ ∎ ∎ ∎ ∎ ∎ ∎ ∎ ∎

Laws and judicial decisions promote inclusion.

by some international educators to be a foolish and radical educational entitlement). No point going back to the days prior to 1975 when children with special needs were not welcomed in our public schools. Prior to the Education of Handicapped Children Act (later renamed Individuals with Disabilities Act or IDEA), many parents had to locate private educational facilities as well as pick up the bill to have their children with special needs educated!

Suffice it to say that after 1975 and the passage of the Education of Handicapped Children Act, for a period of approximately 15–20 years, special education not only came into being, it flourished. Indeed, it grew until we seemed to have a dual system of education, one for "normal" children and one for children with "special needs." Special services, programs, staffing and locations seemed to be the preferred answer to the educational needs of those with disabilities. Teachers, administrators, school districts and even many parents and students accepted and expected a more segregated manner of education for children with special needs. If the truth were known, some still do, but certainly not all.

Those of you who follow educational law may have noted that the term "inclusion" is not written into any of the laws. If such is the case, you might ask, why is inclusion so widespread? The answer is twofold: Powerful lobbies and judicial rulings. Many parents of special needs children who

FYI

The federal government greatly determines how, who and where students will be educated. In 1975 the Education of Handicapped Children Act, otherwise known as the EHCA or PL 94-142, was passed, causing a great shift in the right to access public education. This landmark law ensured that all children were entitled to free public education.

Over the years, attitudes and expectations changed, and by 1997 the Individuals with Disabilities Education Act, IDEA, was passed by Congress, Then in 2002 it was reauthorized (rewritten and extended). This legislation forced changes in servicing and educating children with special needs, redirecting the focus from access to special education to access to general education (Zigmond, 2001).

were segregated for their education felt strongly that their children were being discriminated against and not provided with equal educational opportunities. Moreover, the federal courts have ruled that access to general education is a moral and civil right, in addition to an educational expectation. Our judicial system has paved the way for increasing inclusion through the outcome of test cases, underscoring the right of children to be educated in the least restrictive environment of public education with nondisabled peers.

Consequently, American public education has undergone another transformative shift. Today special education provided in a separate location (separate school, wing or classroom) is deemed undesirable, whereas special educational services given in the general education setting is considered desirable.

"Our judicial system has paved the way for increasing inclusion through the outcome of test cases."

Why inclusion?

Think about it for a minute. Probably the best way to understand the powerful forces behind inclusion is to consider your own situation. Remember when you were new to your job, much like Teresa? Suppose that instead of being welcomed, supported and shown how, when and why to do things, you were left isolated. Even during your lunch break, established cliques ignored you and turned away from your social and professional efforts to join them. You were miserably alone. Initially you thought that being new was the reason. But as time passed and you continued to be excluded, you began to suspect that there was something wrong with you. I think you would agree that such a scenario would probably leave you unhappy, with unhealthy thoughts and less than optimal performance. Exclusion is negative and hurtful.

Inclusion is more than a philosophical term or an educational issue in need of resolution. Indeed, inclusion is a state of mind and a state of being. Perception of worth is partially rooted in how others perceive us.

bottom line
■ ■ ■ ■ ■ ■ ■ ■ ■ ■

Professional survival requires knowledge of current educational law.

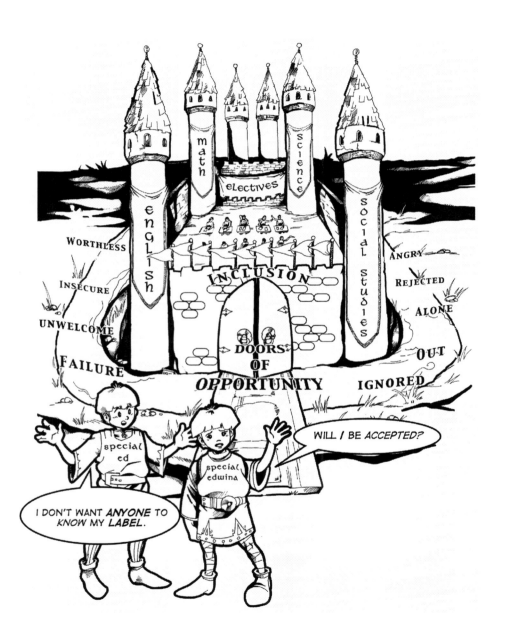

Think about how it feels to be:

Included	*Excluded*
"In"	"Out"
A participant	A nonparticipant
Part of the group	Left out
Happy	Angry
Confident	Uncertain
Valued	Worthless
Secure	Insecure
Given opportunity	At a dead end
Respected	Disrespected
Successful	Failing
Accepted	Rejected
Welcome	Unwelcome
Invited	Ignored

Educators often make the claim that "all children can learn," a notion almost all of us feel comfortable embracing. That being the case, it is perhaps easier to accept the following reasons behind the thrust for inclusion:

- Studies revealed that a disproportionate numbers of males and minorities were placed in special education.

- The behavior and performance of students with special needs improved when they had academically able and behaviorally appropriate students as role models.

- In segregated special education classes the curriculum often differed and educational and behavioral standards were lower than in the general education environment, thereby denying students with special needs equal educational opportunity.

- Parents noted that their children felt left out and excluded in their segregated environment. They expressed concern about unhealthy emotional, social and academic development.

- Society does not segregate special needs people; why should schools?

- Economic and vocational opportunities were limited by classification and education in special education settings.

bottom line
■ ■ ■ ■ ■ ■ ■ ■ ■ ■

Revised Serenity Prayer for inclusion teachers: Grant us the serenity to accept the things we cannot change, the courage to change the things we can and the wisdom to know the difference!

- Students reported hopelessness about their future. Dropout rates and failure rates were of great concern.

- Many educators recognized that separate was not equal.

- The dual system of education was very expensive and unwieldy, with dismayingly poor educational outcomes.

Who will be included?

The answer to this question is ultimately determined by whoever is responsible for interpreting the elastic legal clauses of "least restrictive environment" and "to the maximum extent appropriate." Who really wields the authority in your school and your school district?

In my experience, "leadership" sets the tone for inclusion decision-making. One of my colleagues suggested truthfully that in her elementary school, the decision seemed to be based on expediency: What would be the easiest way to meet federal and state mandates and cause the least amount of change? I suspect her situation is not that atypical.

BRIGHT IDEA

When you consider your roster of students, try not to affix labels to any student. Certainly resist any temptation to speak in a disparaging manner about special education or about students with special needs. Every student has special needs, whether classified or not, and is entitled to your respect and support. Each person performs best in a welcoming and warm environment. Getting to know and appreciate the uniqueness of each child will help you develop a relationship that encourages positive growth.

bottom line

Use your school's existing inclusion framework to help you communicate with parents and students about inclusion.

Local leadership decisions about inclusion, indeed even Committees on Special Education decisions regarding placement of students with special needs, are influenced by school culture. Inclusion detractors, whether administrators, teachers or parents, will impact on the choices made and on the entire inclusion environment. Make no mistake; there are opponents to inclusion, in particular, full inclusion. Parents and educators often complain that a disproportionate amount of human and financial resources are expended on a small percentage of students with special needs, thereby shortchanging the majority of students and, indirectly, society as a whole.

When the primary consideration is not the development of *each* child's potential, inclusion decisions may be determined by such supporting issues as finances, scheduling, staff training and capability (or lack of), and staff and parental pressures. In some cases, compliance with legal mandates can result in "full inclusion," with a school district embracing the concept as well as *all* the youngsters with special needs. All are returned to the local school setting and educated in the general education setting.

Professional journals offer insight into the myriad perspectives of students, parents and staff on inclusion. Issues discussed include the effects of inclusion on nondisabled peers; the academic, social and behavioral gains of the included; and teachers' acceptance of inclusion. Salend, Duhaney and Laurel (1999) provide an overview and extensive bibliography that may be of interest to you.

Generally speaking, philosophical and professional acceptance of *full* inclusion is the exception rather than the rule. Left to their own devices, many school districts and educators would prefer to include those children who are least disabled and continue to exclude those at the fringes— particularly children classified as emotionally disturbed or seriously cognitively or physically impaired.

Nevertheless, federal and state funding formulas encourage the Regular Education Initiative and require detailed reports specifying the extent of compliance, along with justification for exclusion. Consequently, it seems safe to assume that inclusion will continue and probably increase rather than decrease. Further, it is probably safe to say that the expectation of increased inclusion will be obvious in the reauthorization terms of IDEA and that the new legal mandate will reflect the latest research and thinking on improving education for all children.

If your colleagues are much like mine, they probably will confess to a preference for working with the highly motivated, high performing child who, they feel, would

bottom line
■ ■ ■ ■ ■ ■ ■ ■ ■ ■

Inclusion is increasing nationwide, in spite of uncertainty and some confusion.

cause fewer problems, allow for more "traditional" teaching and result in higher academic scores. Many would prefer not to gamble on their professional success in an inclusion class, especially in light of the following:

- Teachers are now held accountable for student progress or lack thereof.

- Professional evaluations can be contingent on positive student academic as well as behavioral results.

- Continued employment might be determined by student success or failure.

- Class report cards are published on the Web and in local newspapers.

Needless to say, in today's inclusionary school environment teachers of inclusion classes have to expect an even wider range of abilities and disabilities in their classrooms than previously. Fortunately, most teachers with whom I have worked expressed confidence in their ability to meet the new challenges, given a supportive environment. These teachers see inclusion as a challenge rather than a problem, even an opportunity to improve their skills and techniques. These same teachers, however, never fail to emphasize that support is essential. At the same time, even the ardent supporters of inclusion admit to being anxious about their ability to teach effectively while meeting the needs of the child labeled emotionally disturbed (ED), behaviorally disordered (BD) or seriously emotionally disabled (SED) and prefer that a child so labeled not be placed in their class.

FYI

Most educators feel that inclusion without the appropriate student and staff support is a recipe for failure. Carefully crafted inclusion programs are student centered and incorporate intensive staff development and administrative support. Educators are concerned about providing strategies, materials and mandated curricular modifications appropriate to the special needs student without sacrificing the high standards appropriate to the general education student. (ERIC Review: Inclusion, 1996)

How might inclusion impact students with special needs?

As you might imagine, the effects of inclusion on the child with special needs is extremely individual. However, perhaps the impact of inclusion can best be seen in stories like that of Ronny, a child from a single-parent home who had a history of considerable emotional and physical abuse from successive foster parents. In fourth grade, Ronny was placed with Ms. S in a special education setting. Ms. S described herself as a demanding "control" kind of person, one who believes that good teachers have a class of silent students who never question teaching authority. She admittedly could not handle Ronny's "uncontrollable behavior" and proclaimed him dangerous to herself and the other students. At his annual review before the Committee on Special Education (CSE), she insisted that, due to his classification as emotionally disturbed and his explosive behavior, he not be considered a candidate for inclusion. Following the CSE's acceptance of Ms. S's recommendation, Ronny was retained in the special class and thereafter refused to do class work. His classmates began to taunt him for his failure to "earn" inclusion status. His behavior deteriorated to the point that explosive outbursts became the norm, not the exception. Ms. S and Ronny both seemed relieved to have the year come to a close.

The next year Ronny's fifth grade special education teacher, Mr. Lingle, had a totally different teaching approach

Federal law defines the SED student as one with any of the following:

- An inability to learn that cannot be explained by intellectual, sensory or other health factors.
- An inability to build or maintain satisfactory interpersonal relationships with peers and teachers.
- Inappropriate types of behavior or feelings under normal circumstances.
- A general pervasive mood of unhappiness or depression.
- A tendency to develop physical symptoms or fears associated with personal or school problems.

The SED term also includes children who are schizophrenic, but does not include children who are socially maladjusted unless it is determined that they have one of the above five characteristics. (Individuals with Disabilities Act, 1997)

bottom line
■ ■ ■ ■ ■ ■ ■ ■ ■ ■

ED is the most underrepresented of all the disabilities of special education.

and response to Ronny. He recognized that Ronny had trust issues as well as difficulty focusing long enough to complete assignments. Further, he noticed that if Ronny was not allowed some latitude in movement, he became a discipline problem for himself, his peers and certainly the teacher. Mr. Lingle made a point of consistently and quietly acknowledging Ronny when his behavior and academic performance were appropriate. After the first quarter of the year, he recommended that Ronny be included for the remainder of the year. Together they worked with the general education teacher and a new set of general education classmates. Together they were able to complete the school year in harmony. By the end of fifth grade, Ronny had passing scores. Better yet, he could be seen in the hall and on the playground with a smile and had even made a few friends with whom to share recess and after-school activities.

"Special ed students in an inclusion setting may find inconsistent supports, higher standards and unaccepting peers."

No, we cannot draw definitive conclusions from this one child, especially with so many variables—different teachers, techniques, attitudes, training and personalities. Also, the difference in Ronnie's age and maturity and, perhaps, improved home circumstances may have contributed to changes, but perhaps not. Many studies indicate that the more normal the environment, the more normal the behavior. Certainly, it appeared that being socially accepted as "one of the guys" rather than a called a "retard" in a special class did a lot for Ronnie. Further, it was obviously an improvement for him academically to accept the assistance of teachers that resulted in completed class work and passing grades. Likewise, it seems obvious that no one wants to feel like a reject, a "retard" or a misfit. Such painful, disparaging descriptors are a lesson to a child that is bound to result in long-term negative fruit.

bottom line
■ ■ ■ ■ ■ ■ ■ ■ ■ ■

Teacher and student success are interdependent.

The Ronny story is only part of the whole. Other included special needs students will react differently, especially children accustomed to a safe, protective special education environment with one-on-one support. As a result of inclusion, they may find themselves in a general education setting with inconsistent supports and higher standards and with peers who may or may not be accepting. Just as you might expect, student response is very much dependent on the environment teachers provide and the acceptance and support both teachers and students offer.

How might inclusion impact non–special needs students?

Sometimes we get so caught up with the who, how and why aspects of inclusion and the special needs child that we tend to overlook the fact that change in placement results in change for all, including the non–special needs students, staff and parents. There is no denying that in these challenging educational times, many classroom teachers are not enthusiastic about having to handle more challenges. Some are already having difficulty with the social and legal mandate to raise academic standards no matter what the situation, especially with school and classroom results published on websites and in newspapers. The teacher's professional expertise and positive attitude are critical when it comes to effective classroom management and high quality educational programs for all students.

 **LEGAL ALERT**

A new federally funded research service is now available to educators. The purpose of this online site is to provide professionals with accurate information of what *really* works in education, based on accurate scientific research. Since the newest federal legislation (No Child Left Behind) mandates that programs be research based, this site should be helpful reading. Check out the site at www.whatworks.ed.gov. (Viadero, 2004)

Academic implications

There is no point in claiming that inclusion will simplify the teacher's role and make attainment of curricular objectives more forthcoming when it just isn't so. Parents or guardians of non–special needs students, as well as the students themselves, will continue to have high expectations and demand a rigorous academic program. Such being the case, the need is obvious for more teaching precision, greater subject matter expertise and a well-developed classroom management repertoire. Fortunately, federal and state education departments are mandating that school districts

bottom line
■ ■ ■ ■ ■ ■ ■ ■ ■ ■

Inclusion is most effective when coteaching teams are volunteers.

implement staff development programs to assist the teacher. Also, professional online websites offer assistance in every aspect of teaching: Curriculum development, teaching techniques, behavior management, classroom and curricular materials and burn-out prevention strategies. Later chapters in this book will give you practical tips to make your work easier and more effective. You will also find the websites listed at the back of the book helpful as you search for ways to become more skilled in your teaching.

Behavioral and social implications

It can be a formidable task for a teacher to establish and maintain a safe, encouraging learning environment that will have a positive impact on all students. Let us not forget that enthusiastic, dedicated professionals have already been doing that for many years. The greatest concern for the non–special needs student seems to result from those included students who exhibit acting-out behaviors or require almost constant one-on-one assistance to remain on task. Increasingly, safety concerns are being addressed legislatively in efforts to ensure that teachers and school principals will not have to worry about dangerous students threatening the well-being of students or staff. (This issue of discipline is addressed in depth in Chapter 6.)

FYI

Research indicates that included special needs students show more normalized social development and interaction as well as enhanced skill acquisition, improved health and attendance, and greater all-around success. At the same time, studies show that such inclusion provides classmates with more positive attitudes about disabilities. (Lombardi, 1999)

Potently, let us also not overlook a positive aspect of an inclusive environment in our multi-ethnic global society—providing students with opportunities to interact with and treat all people with respect and dignity.

Legal implications

Access to information has become so much easier for parents, students and teachers, thanks to the Internet. The concerned parent with a desire to be well informed can be a blessing or a threat to you. Many of your parents will be familiar with the following terms and expect you to be as well. I am a firm believer in "an ounce of prevention is worth a pound of cure" and, consequently, I suggest you familiarize yourself with these terms (or keep them handy for quick consult) in preparation for your teacher-parent relationships.

504 Section 504 of the Rehabilitation Act of 1973 covers all students with mental or physical impairments that affect a major life function (ADD/ADHD are prime examples). A student classified as 504 may or may not display characteristics similar to a special education student and may have similar accommodations provided for instruction. It is important for teachers to be aware of this legislation because 504 accommodation plans, in particular, discipline plans and intervention plans, preempt a school district's regular disciplinary code.

BRIGHT IDEA

If you are involved in inclusion, be on the lookout for alerts that will impact your teaching methods and classroom strategies. Check your roster to identify any 504 students or students with other special needs. Take time to familiarize yourself with IEPs, BIPs, 504 accommodation plans and testing modifications. If you need clarification, ask a school psychologist. Bear in mind that BIP strategies may help you deal with behavior issues of non–special needs students! (Stride, 2004)

BD/ED/SED Behaviorally disturbed (BD), emotionally disabled (ED) and severely emotionally disturbed/disabled (SED) are terms used in different states to describe the student with behavioral or emotional responses so abnormal (compared with appropriate age, cultural or societal norms) as to adversely affect educational performance.

BIP A behavior intervention plan is a statement of strategies and supports to assist the student with disabilities who has problem behaviors. It must be included in the student's IEP. A BIP must be proactive and multidimensional and should be followed by all teachers of that student.

CSE The Committee on Special Education is a group of individuals involved in the education of the child with

bottom line
■ ■ ■ ■ ■ ■ ■ ■ ■ ■

Keep an open mind and open eyes in your search for new strategies to help you improve your teaching.

special needs who discuss the child's needs, assess progress or lack of it and draw up an appropriate educational and behavioral plan. Participants invited to attend the CSE meetings include the parents, the child (where appropriate), the special education teacher and the general education teacher involved in the provision of education. The chairperson of the CSE meeting may be a psychologist or school administrator who knows the child.

IDEA authorizes school officials to seek temporary removal of a dangerous student (one who brings drugs or weapons to school, or possesses, uses or sells drugs at a school function). An impartial hearing officer can order the student to an Interim Alternative Educational Setting (IAES) for up to 45 days. School officials are permitted to use long-term disciplinary measures when it has been determined that the misbehavior is not related to the disability. In such a case, the consequence of the misbehavior may be commensurate with that for the nondisabled student. Whenever a student is excluded for at least 10 cumulative days, educational services must be continued. (Yell, Rozalski & Drasgow, 2001)

IAES   An interim alternative educational setting, such as home tutoring or suspension, may be used with students with disabilities to the same extent that they are used with the general population, provided they are short-term placements (up to 10 cumulative days). Administrators can remove a student with disabilities who is a threat to self, to others or to a safe and orderly school environment without a manifestation determination, an IEP team meeting or permission from parents. However, they *must* inform students and parents of due process rights.

IDEA/FAPE   The Individuals with Disabilities Education Act (IDEA), reauthorized in 1997, ensures the Free and Public Education (FAPE) of all children and youth. A newer version of IDEA has passed both houses of Congress and is currently being reviewed in Congressional committee for yet another reauthorization. Stay tuned for the new version sometime in 2005, probably expanded and modified.

IEP   The Individualized Educational Plan is a legal document prepared annually, usually by special educators with input from general educators involved in the child's education. The document includes pertinent student data: The disability;

bottom line
■ ■ ■ ■ ■ ■ ■ ■ ■ ■

IDEA does not prevent schools from disciplining ED students; it does attempt to prevent unfair treatment.

the services to be provided; any testing modifications; and the behavioral, academic and transitional objectives set forth for the year. The IEP is expected to be available to all persons who provide services to the child.

LRE   The least restrictive environment is the placement, designated by the CSE and written into the student's IEP, in which the student will receive instruction. According to IDEA, state legislation and court rulings, students are expected to be educated, as much as possible, in the general education environment.

Manifestation Determination   This procedure involves a review of a special education student's misconduct to determine whether or not it is a manifestation of the student's disability. Law states that positive behavioral interventions, support and services must be provided and written into the IEP for students who exhibit severe behavioral problems. Further, before instituting long-term suspension, expulsion or change in placement, the school (usually the CSE) determines whether the student's IEP is appropriate and whether behavioral supports have been provided. School administrators must ascertain that teachers understand and follow any intervention or disciplinary procedures set forth in an IEP, a 504 accommodation plan or a BIP.

BRIGHT IDEA

You will want to promote the opportunity for the special needs student to succeed by using the mandated accommodation, and you know by law you must. But be careful not to overdo it. Students need to learn how to maximize their talents and skills to overcome their disability. They should not be encouraged to become dependent on unnecessary support, much as you would never encourage a mobile person to use a motorized wheelchair!

bottom line

Let IDEA and NCLB laws help you improve education for all students.

NCLB   The No Child Left Behind Act was passed in 2002 with the intent of closing achievement gaps and significantly improving the achievement of all students. This federal legislation renews and updates the Elementary and Secondary Education Act, originally passed in 1965. The law incorporates four major goals: (1) accountability for results, (2) use of strategies and materials that have been scientifically proven to produce results, (3) more parental options and (4) increased local control and flexibility.

REI   The regular education initiative, or the inclusion education movement as part of general education reform, is the movement to return special education students to general classroom environments for instruction with age- and grade-appropriate peers.

Test modifications   Test modifications for special education students are granted to students whose disabilities are severe enough to require a "level playing field" for taking exams. These special accommodations may include extended time, a special location, a scribe, having directions or questions read and using a word processor. These modifications must be established by the Committee on Special Education, included in the student's Individual Education Plan and provided by all school staff.

Power of ⊙ne

The Challenge

Mrs. Blaine, a veteran teacher considered by her peers to be a "master teacher," admitted her frustration with the handling of inclusion in her elementary school. "As little as I know about inclusion, I can see that the casual manner in which it is done in our school is going to beget problems. Teachers know next to nothing about how to do it or what it really means. I admit that I'm one of the ignorant ones. This year we will have two new inclusion classes, and we are all in the dark about their impact. I can't help but think I might be involved next. What can I do to prepare myself?"

The Response

Mrs. Blaine has a vested interest in the whole school attitude, environment and manner in which inclusion is conducted. But, truly, her initial focus has to be on her own preparation and response to inclusion. No matter how dedicated she is, some decisions and policies are simply outside her power base. Mrs. Blaine has identified her own needs, and that is where she should start, educating herself and keeping open to new ideas and new strategies. Her success (and that of her students) starts in her classroom. One teacher and one classroom can work, even in the midst of external chaos or confusion.

SURVEY OF SCHOOL'S INCLUSION READINESS

Answering the following questions will help you prepare for successful inclusion.

1. What position do school administrators take regarding inclusion? To teachers? to students? to parents? Is this position written? spoken? assumed?

2. What official notification has there been about inclusion to the staff? the PTA? the community? the student body?

3. How does the ancillary staff (cafeteria workers, bus drivers, secretaries, custodians, security guards, etc.) treat special education students?

4. What does your school handbook say about special education and inclusion?

5. What inclusion workshops or other staff development opportunities are available in your district or county?

6. What videos or other support resources are in your school or professional library?

7. Who are the school or district psychologists? What hours or periods during the day are they available? Where are their offices? What are their phone numbers?

8. What position does the health office or nursing staff take in regard to distributing medication to students? What procedure is suggested to the teacher who has a student taking medication?

9. What is your school crisis plan for students exhibiting violent behavior or abuse? What steps are you expected to take?

10. What resource staff (guidance counselor, psychologist, social worker, nurse, dean of students) are available for emergency assistance to students during the class period? What is the recommended procedure for arranging an emergency visit by a student?

2

Getting Started

ONLY THE BRIGHT,
THE WELL MANNERED
AND THE CLEAN?

Alan, the fourth grade lead teacher, pushed open the door to the teacher's lounge and stood in the doorway for a minute looking around. In truth he wished he could be someplace else. Assaulted by the raised voices and obvious anger spewing forth, he thought, "Wouldn't it be great if someone sold a product that would repel negativity?" He really did not want to cross the threshold but knew he was expected.

"Well, look who's here! Our 'all-knowing' lead teacher has finally arrived!" one of Alan's fourth grade coteachers, Jessica, loudly pronounced. The smile on her face did nothing to hide her sarcasm.

Alan grinned, decided to not to respond to Jessica and eased into one of the few empty chairs. It appeared that all of the upper elementary teachers had decided to come to the impromptu meeting. "Not bad," he reflected, "at least they feel strongly enough to come and speak up." That thought was quickly replaced with, "Wait a minute, they have always been good

"Inclusion provokes strong reactions, many of which may be fear-induced."

at speaking up." He determined to just sit and watch for a bit to see which teachers were talking and which were listening. "Most important," thought Alan, "let me find out who people are listening to."

Angry comments continued to charge the room. Alan wondered when and if anyone with another point of view would speak out.

"It's ridiculous. That's what it is. How can administration expect us to meet the new standards *and* to take more handicapped students into our classes?"

"You said it. They load up our classes with problem children and then at the end of the year, we look like the ones who failed."

Alan remained silent, hoping someone would counter the thoughts and feelings that permeated the room. Perhaps he would have to be the one to represent the opposition again.

Just as Alan was about to give up hope that some other teacher would speak a bit more positively, Lavinia entered the conversation. Her well-modulated and quiet voice demanded attention: "Excuse me, my friends, but are we not teachers? Isn't that what we elected to do, to teach children who need our help? I don't remember being told that I could pick and choose my students or that I could elect to teach only the bright and well mannered, the personable and the clean. I suggest that we need to rethink how we proceed with the inclusion challenge."

bottom line

■ ■ ■ ■ ■ ■ ■ ■ ■ ■

"Hold yourself responsible for a higher standard than anybody else expects of you. Never excuse yourself."—Henry Ward Beecher

Maybe you are not an Alan, or even a Lavinia. No, we are not all meant to be leaders. Sometimes the best we can do is merely do the best we can at what we are expected to do. At other times, if we take our values seriously, we have to speak out and offer what might be an unpopular, even conflicting, viewpoint. Inclusion is one of those educational issues that provokes strong reactions, many of which may be fear-induced. Alan realized that due to his position of leadership, teachers could pretty much anticipate his stance. He suspected that if he butted in too quickly, he would be resented for opposing their views. He also figured that it would be more effective and productive if a respected coteacher redirected thinking in a positive direction, allowing him the role of guiding action as needed.

The mindset

Teaching remains a profession where you have a lot of latitude regarding what transpires "on the job," in your classroom. You set the tone; you set the physical, academic and emotional environment. Yes, I agree, teaching is not what it used to be, but nothing is! The standards are increasingly being raised, as is your accountability. But think what a marvelous opportunity you have to guide young minds in a positive direction, to help build academic skills, to encourage young people to become responsible, kind and helpful. After all, your students spend more time with you during a school day than with any other adult in their life. Your posture, your facial expression, your attitude, your expectations and your every word will affect each student every day, and maybe well beyond the year they share with you. Your mindset, believe it or not, is the most powerful part of your credentials and professionalism.

A review of reading instruction in inclusion classes underscored that successful student learning was greatly dependent on teacher attitudes. Teacher beliefs, combined with teacher-student collaboration, shaped the context for successful and effective reading instruction. (Schmidt et al., 2002)

You may say to yourself, "Well, this is supposed to be a book on inclusion, so why don't we get on with the essentials?" Trust me, this is definitely about inclusion and this is definitely about essentials. Your mindset is the key not only to surviving inclusion but, potently, to succeeding with inclusion. If you decide that inclusion won't work, it won't. If you continually talk negatively and think negatively, your behavior and attitude will project the same negativity. If you decide that inclusion can work, you will find a way to make it work. You will search out others who think similarly, and you will open your mind to innovative techniques, models and materials to refine your teaching. With a positive mind, you will be receptive to opportunities for professional growth.

The intent of this book is to help you make inclusion work, to help you and all your students succeed in the classroom. Indeed, inclusion challenges us to find ways to work smarter, to be more creative and certainly to benefit from the ideas and strategies that have worked for others. You are not in this alone! You cannot afford to be alone. In this chapter, the focus will be on inclusion models and collaboration. I will show you inclusion models that are now in use in classrooms nationwide. These models will help you envision how to structure your day and use methods that may differ from what you are accustomed to. Furthermore, I hope to save you frustration and time by suggesting ways to get off on the right foot in your coteaching experience.

"Most inclusion decisions will be made for you, without your input."

School culture is a very distinctive thing, an often-neglected factor that powerfully influences both student and staff success. Certainly this is true for inclusion. How inclusion will affect the staff and students in your school is directly dependent on the size and finances of your school as well as the flexibility and experience of your leadership. Attitudes and behaviors of ancillary staff, as well as professional staff, have a potent affect on the school environment and most definitely on the treatment of special needs students. They can either positively or negatively impinge on inclusion efforts.

No doubt, in talking with professionals from other schools, you noted that schools seem to respond to federal and state demands in their own manner and to develop an operational style unique to their particular resources. Elementary schools often operate quite differently from each other in terms of both organizational structure and delivery of services to students.

bottom line
■ ■ ■ ■ ■ ■ ■ ■ ■ ■

If you always do what you've always done, you'll always get what you always got.

Now, about the all-important decision of how inclusion will occur in your school. The truth is that most inclusion decisions will be made *for you*, without your input. The decisions will no doubt result in guidelines by which you will be expected to operate and abide. Few individual teachers have developed a large enough or influential enough powerbase to impact on such a major school decision as how inclusion will be implemented. (However, that may be something you want to think about in terms of your future professional networking!)

Okay, so let's say you found out you have been scheduled for an inclusion class this year. Let's say you know little about what that means in terms of what you have always done and how you have done it and how things will change. You do not doubt that things will change, but you wonder how much *you* will have to change.

Inclusion models

The leadership in many school districts realizes that transitioning from special education as a place (students educated in a special setting) to special education as a service (students serviced in the general setting) requires intensive support for teachers and students. Consequently, coteaching or collaborative team teaching has become a popular district response. It is one of the most written about and popular responses to inclusion, perhaps because it offers the opportunity to provide the most support to classroom efforts. It is an expensive option because it is staff-intensive and demands ongoing staff development and shared planning time to promote success.

Later in this chapter we will also look at the collaborating consultant coteaching model, a cost effective option to coteach successfully.

The collaborative coteaching model

Generally speaking, in the collaborative coteaching model two teachers work together to teach a class of mixed special education and general education students. The general education teacher is considered the subject expert, and the special education teacher, the specialist. Let's assume that your school has elected to use this instructional model. The following table shows five operating alternatives for two teachers working in the same classroom for the purpose of whole group instruction. Bear in mind that this collaborative

bottom line
■ ■ ■ ■ ■ ■ ■ ■ ■ ■

"The person who makes no mistakes does not usually make anything."—
Edward J. Phelps

Option	How it works	Potential benefits	Potential liabilities
One teaches, one circulates	One teacher takes responsibility for instruction. The other moves throughout the classroom assisting students, correcting assignments and monitoring behavior.	■ Help can be provided to students as needed. ■ Behavior difficulties can be dealt with prior to escalation. ■ The circulating teacher can assess the extent to which students grasp subject matter.	■ Physical layout must permit circulation. ■ Circulation can interfere with lecture or demonstration. ■ If circulating teacher remains in that role, students tend to see her as an unequal partner.
One teaches; one reteaches.	One teacher takes responsibility for the initial instruction. The other teacher further explains, demonstrates or rewords the instruction as needed.	■ Can be effective with all language impaired (ESL) as well as special education students. ■ Provides another informational pathway; should improve knowledge retention.	■ Requires ongoing collaborative planning for the re-teaching to be effective. ■ In high stakes situations, this option can be time-consuming. ■ May raise issues with more talented students about the stigma of special education.
One teaches; one supports	One teacher takes responsibility for instruction; the other supports with computer programs, AV, DVD, etc., as well as with disciplinary control.	■ Allows opportunity for multimodal approach, effectively teaching to many learning styles. ■ Relieves teaching member for seeking out or constructing additional resources. ■ Teaching member controls subject matter in initial presentation. ■ With strong, trusting collaborative team, can be very effective in enhancing instruction for all.	■ Unequal teaching status because the teaching member "controls." ■ Students may perceive supporting teacher as less than a teacher, ignoring input and disciplinary attempts. ■ Coteachers must work hard to develop a team that can really collaborate.

Option	How it works	Potential benefits	Potential liabilities
Share and share alike.	Both members assume responsibility for teaching after coteaching planning. Responsibilities for lessons or portions of lessons may be assigned and rotated as plans specify. Responsibility for discipline is shared.	▪ Both teachers must be prepared and knowledgeable. ▪ Both teachers have equal status with students. ▪ Instructional responsibility is divided, and instructional performance can be amplified. ▪ Coteachers responsible for *all* students. ▪ Reduces resentment regarding the burden of responsibility and instruction.	▪ Both teachers must feel and act like a team. ▪ Teacher rapport is essential. ▪ Success depends on preparation and trust. ▪ Some teachers fear relinquishing any control. ▪ Shared planning time is essential.
Superteacher and invisible teacher.	One member assumes complete responsibility for instruction and behavior. One member is virtually nonparticipating.	▪ The controlling member maintains complete authority for whatever occurs or does not occur in the classroom. ▪ The more knowledgeable teacher can present an accurate and challenging lesson without being concerned about on-task behavior. ▪ The teaching member can benefit from input from the observing teacher.	▪ Waste of taxpayer money and the talent of the second teacher. ▪ Both members wonder why there are two teachers in the room. ▪ Needs of students are not met effectively. ▪ Students disregard the nonparticipating teacher as less than a qualified teacher. ▪ Resentment builds to the detriment of the relationship.

coteaching relationship may be for the full school day or for only a specific period.

These five alternatives allow for choice in the collaborative coteaching model for large group instruction. Hopefully, you and your coteacher will select options that promote student growth academically and behaviorally. However, since much

Model	How it works
Parallel teaching	Collaborating teachers split the class, and each instructs a portion of the class based on student skill levels. The split is not meant to be static or based on classification but rather on specific need related to subject area or skill. The same lesson is taught utilizing the same materials.
Station teaching	The lesson is divided into halves. Each collaborating teacher specializes in a portion and teaches to half the class. Instructors rotate so that the entire lesson is delivered to both parts of the class.
Remedial instruction	One of the teachers, usually the general educator, offers challenging or advanced instruction to a portion of the class. The other, usually the special educator, uses specialized materials and methods to remediate earlier instruction. Strategies, pacing, vocabulary and focus may be at a less demanding level.
Supplemental instruction	One of the teachers, usually the general educator, presents the lesson. The other, usually the special educator, simplifies or extends concepts for those needing further explanation and help.
Concurrent instruction	One of the teachers, usually the general educator, presents the introductory part of the lesson. Both teachers share in assisting with remediation, supplementation or extension of the lesson.
Cooperative learning group instruction	The class is divided into small groups of varying ability to complete given assignments and to learn different group work roles. Teachers organize, supervise and guide the groups to work toward established goals.

(Stride, 2004; Cook & Friend, 1995)

teaching is done in small groups let's next consider different models for doing small group instruction collaboratively.

Flexibility and choices—for large and small group instruction—are essential for successful collaboration. You and your new partner have lots of different paths you might take on your journey toward academic success for all of your students. I suspect that until you meet and get to know and trust your coteacher, you will be unable to determine a model appropriate to both of your teaching styles. Some teachers feel it very helpful to develop and agree on a contract before meeting students (see Chapter 5).

Do not feel overwhelmed or dismayed because of uncertainty. It may be that one option works well for you, another for your partner. It may be that you use one model now, and as you become more familiar and reliant on each other, another model seems more effective later. It may be that for a particular lesson one option fits your needs, but for another lesson you select a different option. It is important to open your mind to discovery, change and awareness of how personality, talents and learning styles impact on choice. Moreover, you may find that your students influence your decisions. Some will thrive with techniques that turn other students off. Together you and your coteacher should thoughtfully consider, experiment and evaluate the different alternatives. You may even want to involve your students in helping you with your decision-making!

Having co-taught in inclusion settings for several years, I have had a myriad of wonderful, disappointing and unusual experiences, all of which have contributed one way or another to my professional growth. Personally, I am most comfortable with sharing responsibility, sharing authority,

BRIGHT IDEA

Make a special effort to listen, really listen, to your new coteaching collaborator. Get your relationship off to a positive start by promising yourself not to interrupt, change the subject or put down ideas. Listen with your eyes, your ears and your body! Just as your students need to know you care, so does your teaching partner. Affirming worth by listening builds trust—the basis of a good collaborative relationship.

bottom line
■ ■ ■ ■ ■ ■ ■ ■ ■ ■

"Our greatest glory is not in never falling, but in rising every time we fall."— *Confucius* and sharing success and failure of all students. I can also tell you I have been placed in collaborating situations where my coteacher felt it impossible to relinquish any control.

One June I was notified that Mr. Summers and I would be collaborating in an inclusion science class the following year. I felt a measure of relief for two reasons: (1) I was told in advance about the collaborating relationship rather than the first day of school, and (2) Mr. Summers and I had gotten along well together personally and professionally. His low-key attitude was appealing. Although I had never seen him teach, I felt confident that we would develop into a strong collaborating team.

In one of our initial planning sessions, Mr. Summers spoke with me about his teaching plan that he claimed was "foolproof."I am generally suspicious of claims for foolproof methods, but I wanted to remain open-minded. Before long, I recognized that his foolproof plan was built on lecture, videos and dittos. He talked in a monotone. He followed up with worksheets that were so boring the students were too busy daydreaming to cause disciplinary problems. I suspect that was why he claimed he had a foolproof teaching plan. Come to think of it, in all fairness, his description could not be faulted because never did he describe his plan using words such as individualized, relevant or exciting.

bottom line
■ ■ ■ ■ ■ ■ ■ ■ ■ ■

"Learn from the mistakes of others. . . . You won't have time to make them all yourself."— *Anonymous*

To his credit, Mr. Summers agreed to plan with me weekly so that we both were aware of objectives, methods and materials. He was always polite and respectful to me and of my ideas and suggestions, even to the point of making me feel that he might invite me to assist in the incorporation of them. Alas, it never happened. He was not opposed to my finding materials, making copies of dittos or grading papers. He did not want anyone, meaning me, interfering with his daily science lesson nor with his grading system. He definitely did not want me circulating the room while he lectured. He did not want me talking to students while they did assigned seatwork, even to assist them or clarify a point. Students questioned my role and my authority. I did too! In such a situation, a positive mindset is essential to undergird survival and any success.

I share this example with you because my preferred collaborative teaching option and that of Mr. Summers were absolute opposites. Truly, I was as much responsible for the unfortunate collaborative partnership that developed as was Mr. Summers. I knew the subject matter. I had an extensive variety of materials and strategies for a wide range of student abilities and disabilities. But, I had not adequately prepared for the yearlong intimate relationship into which I had knowingly entered. What I did not do was prepare for collaboration. Perhaps you also learn the most from your mistakes. I learned a lot from my misguided efforts to collaborate with Mr. Summers. That year was a powerful learning experience for me. I hope this book can help you avoid similar situations.

Collaborative consultant coteaching model

Quite often elementary schools do not have the resources to allow coteaching for a full period or a full day and instead provide support to the general education teacher through the services of a consultant teacher. The consultant teacher, a special education teacher, is assigned to one or more general educators. This specialist is expected to provide materials, offer advice on strategies and management techniques, discuss IEPs and BIPs, and meet the specific needs of included students.

In this consultant-teaching model, a special education teacher may be assigned to meet the needs of included students and inclusion staff members in several general classes as well as in a variety of subject areas. In fact, a skilled, intuitive professional may render invaluable service to both teachers and special needs students, especially in schools with a low incidence of special needs students or a low total school population. The consultant teacher, a specially trained educator, supports the general educator and the students, often indirectly. Unfortunately, in many cases, what really happens is that general educators find themselves overwhelmed and totally responsible for all students, academically and behaviorally, because consultant teachers may be stretched so thin over so many classes that they are

"The consultant teacher must provide materials, offer advice on strategies, discuss IEPs and BIPs, and meet the specific needs of included students."

bottom line
■ ■ ■ ■ ■ ■ ■ ■ ■ ■

FEAR (false emotions appearing real) is a powerful, usually negative, motivator.

incapable of really supporting anyone effectively. Moreover, because shared planning time in elementary schools may not be a possibility, consulting may have to be done on a "catch as catch can" basis, thereby causing, rather than alleviating, problems.

Some schools elect to handle the "inclusion problem" by using paraprofessionals to support teachers and special needs students. When schools are facing serious staffing or financial shortfalls, it is tempting for them to assign several paraprofessionals or aides instead of a certified teacher to support the inclusion needs in a classroom. In such cases, the general educator really is responsible for the academic and behavioral needs of all the students and for the supervision of the para-educator as well. It's easy to see that clearly defined roles and operating procedures as well as a strong rapport are essential if you hope for instructional and learner support.

BRIGHT IDEA

If you are assigned as a coteacher consultant, make every effort to be accommodating to the general educators. Use your support time wisely. Find out how and when it is best to make regular contact. Find out what will support the general educators and align your services to their needs. If possible, attempt to provide in-class assistance related to academic or behavioral needs.

Aide? Paraprofessional? Many teachers swear that their support is pivotal to their teaching success, offering bilingual assistance, encouraging students and promoting on-task behavior. Be aware, however, that the No Child Left Behind legislation mandates raising the bar for this group of minimally paid individuals. Not only does the law require highly qualified teachers in each classroom, it also impels movement toward assuring that all para-educators have adequate knowledge and skills for instructional support roles.

bottom line

THINK: Is what you say thoughtful, helpful, important, necessary and kind?

When it comes to "assistants," it's important to know your terms because it matters for the type of assistance legally permitted. Bear in mind that in all cases, the teacher must directly supervise any work of paraprofessionals with students. Because the use of paraprofessionals is becoming increasingly important, especially in inclusion settings, I will devote more to this topic in Chapter. 5.

Your new role as a collaborating coteacher in an inclusion class is the beginning of a challenging journey. May the following suggestions help you as you travel on your journey:

LEGAL ALERT

Wrightslaw reminds us that the terms "aides" and "paraprofessionals" are not synonymous. The No Child Left Behind legislation mandates that paraprofessionals have studied a minimum of two years at an institution of higher learning, have earned at least an associate's degree and have met a rigorous standard of quality as demonstrated through a formal academic assessment. There is no legal definition for "aide."

Visit http://www.wrightslaw.com/heath/parapro. aide.htm for more information.

- Focus on *what is,* not on what you *wish* was. Assess your situation from a practical standpoint. Expend your energy on those teaching tasks over which you have control, not administrative decisions over which you have no control.

- Bear in mind that you are not alone. All over the country teachers are dealing with similar challenges, and you can profit from their successes and failures. Thanks to technology, there are many ways to access invaluable information and resources that can help you. Also, do not hesitate to seek ideas, advice and alternatives from professional colleagues in your school setting.

- Focus on the needs of *all* the students, rather than fixate on the special needs students. They are all children first. They all need to be encouraged, enjoyed and supported in learning the curriculum you teach.

- Keep your sense of humor close at hand. Allow yourself to laugh at yourself and your mistakes. Recognize and appreciate your own humanity!

bottom line
■ ■ ■ ■ ■ ■ ■ ■ ■ ■

"Whether you think you can or you think you can't . . . you're right."—*Henry Ford*

- Remember that you decided to be a teacher to reach out to young people. Align your efforts, your expertise and your focus on making a positive difference to all students, even those at the fringes. Take advantage of documents written to help—IEPs and BIPs.

For good beginnings to a collaborative teaching relationship:

- SMILE: Smile, motivate, intuit, listen, energize.

FYI

Educators in this multicultural country need to be attuned to differing cultural habits and expectations. Language patterns, as well as verbal and nonverbal behaviors, affect interpersonal relationships, for teachers as well as students. (Stride, 2004)

The dominant cultural value of Latino, Native American and African American people is cooperation and relationship. In contrast, the North American value system highly prizes individualism and competition. Further, Latinos, Native Americans and African Americans view how goals are reached as being as important as reaching the goal. Emphasis is on "we," whereas the dominant pronoun of North Americans is "I." (Morefield, 1998)

Knowledge and appreciation of divergent cultures is essential in any collaboration.

- Remain flexible. Ask your coteacher for opinions, ideas and techniques. Always be ready to modify approaches, strategies and materials.

- Share your space. Allocate an area for your coteacher's professional and personal belongings. Arrange nonverbal signals for such emergencies as trips to the bathroom, a serious behavior problem, a need for assistance.

- Resist any temptation to be negative to and about your coteacher or any students. Criticism can be helpful only if it is constructive and well intended, not mean-spirited or personal.

- Show your professionalism with the seven B's: Be prompt. Be prepared. Be neat. Be courteous. Be responsible. Be alert to unspoken needs. Be ready to laugh.

Power of 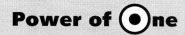ne

The Challenge

Lavinia, a seasoned teacher much revered by colleagues as a "real professional," is a staunch supporter of inclusion. In her usual open manner, she confessed to one serious concern with her involvement: "I've never been in the position to coteach and share my classroom with anyone. I'm not sure I have a clue about helping to make it comfortable for both of us. How will I welcome another teacher when I am uncertain of how they translate their expertise into action? I certainly don't want to start off on the wrong foot!"

The Response

Fortunately for her future coteacher, Lavinia has already decided to do two very important things for collaboration success: Welcome the coteacher and make preparations. The very first contact often sets the tone for the relationship. Take time to develop a warm professional relationship and to show your interest in this new and important person about to share your life. Establish a mutually convenient time for regular planning and evaluation of the stages of your working relationship. Consider using some of the suggested collaborative teaching guides at the end of this chapter as a starting point.

COLLABORATIVE TEACHING
DECISION-MAKING GUIDE

The following questions are meant to be a guide for your coteaching experience. How you and your coteacher respond is important to the everyday functioning of your class. First, answer the questions silently. Next, discuss your answers and determine collaboratively how you will proceed.

Communication issues

1. Which of you will be the "master of ceremonies" and introduce you both to students and parents?

2. How will you explain to students and parents the reason for the coteaching situation? (Caution: Check on how your administration is reporting inclusion in the student handbook and to parents. Adjust your answer accordingly.)

3. Who will communicate with parents?

4. How often and in what manner (letters, phone calls, visitations, emails, Web page on school web site) will you communicate with parents?

5. Who will take responsibility for communicating inclusion needs and successes to administration and colleagues, and how will these be conveyed?

6. When and how often will monitoring and evaluation of the collaborative effort take place (e.g., orally, at weekly planning session)?

Logistical Issues

1. How will the room be arranged for students—desks in rows, circle, groups?

2. Where will coteachers work and keep their professional and personal belongings?

3. How will teacher space be shared?

4. What materials will be used? Where will they be stored?

5. What space will be used for providing extra help or small group work?

6. Who will be responsible for clean-up of the shared space at the end of each class or day.

POSSIBLE ROLES IN
COLLABORATIVE TEACHING

The following roles have generally been assumed by general and special educators. It is my belief that as the coteaching team develops collaboratively, there will be less definite assignment and assumption of responsibility and more blurring of roles. Both teachers will become more knowledgeable and proficient at working with all students.

General educator	Special educator
Curricula expert.	Expert on instructional materials, strategies for diverse needs.
High stakes exam expert.	Expert at dealing with aberrant behavior.
Supervisor of class routines.	Innovative with strategies and curricular development.
Aware of time constraints.	Recognizes potential behavioral conflicts.
Knowledgeable about subject matter, assignments, guidelines.	Knowledgeable about modifying instructional materials, tests, homework assignments.
Familiar with text and resources.	Knows support staff and their helping capabilities; is prepared to seek help as needed.
Cognizant of evaluation techniques for subject areas.	Coordinates CSE meetings, pupil personnel meetings and parent contact.
Aware of behaviors considered "normal."	Expert on special needs students' IEPs, BIPs, test modifications and regulations for implementation.
Has a repertoire of strategies and activities to promote academic success for mainstream students.	Good at developing and personalizing relationships with students.
Knows department personalities and operating procedures.	Ready to individualize assignments as needed.

Enhancing Your Support for Inclusion

IS IT A MISTAKE?

"Hey, Kevin, Jodie's fall schedule arrived in the mail this morning," Emily Sanders said to her husband, who was enjoying a leisurely Saturday brunch.

Kevin, swallowing a bite of sandwich, mumbled, "I can't quite grasp that my baby is old enough to be in sixth grade already."

"You know, Kevin, it looks like Jodie will be having the same teacher that Jordan had. I don't get it. How can that be possible?"

"Well, why not? She'll be in the same school."

"Come on, Kevin, I know you always try to avoid admitting it, but Jodie has been in special education for years. She's always had special education teachers in special classes."

"I think you are going overboard worrying, Emily. So she's got the teacher Jordan had; how is that going to be a problem?"

"Be serious Kevin, do you think for one minute that Jodie will survive academically in the same level of class that Jordan had? That's why I'm worrying. There must be a mistake on her schedule."

This chapter is devoted to a very important aspect of teaching—enlisting parent's assistance and support.

Parents have the right to know about their child's school and educational program. They also have a responsibility to help the school educate their child. To do that, they need to be informed. They need to know expectations. With your help, they will be better prepared for this important shared responsibility.

"Parents have the right to know about their child's educational program and a responsibility to help educate their child."

The Sanders, in the account above, might not know it, but there are big changes involving Jodie's educational placement. As Emily pointed out, Jodie always had special education teachers in special classes. Being an observant mom, she noticed that the teacher to whom Jodie was assigned was not a special education teacher. Being a concerned mom, she wondered what was going on and how it would affect Jodie. Answers for this observant and concerned mother might well center around the educational term "inclusion."

The Sanders, like many parents, may have never heard of inclusion in relation to their child's education. It is a term all parents need to know. For parents with children who seriously need special help to have a shot at academic and social success, the inclusion issue has important ramifications. Face it; *you* may be the person they come to for an explanation. You, as Jodie's teacher, certainly want her parents on your team to help with the responsibility of educating her.

Talking to parents about inclusion

The following issues may be helpful in guiding your parent-teacher discussions:

bottom line
■ ■ ■ ■ ■ ■ ■ ■ ■ ■
Your best efforts are amplified when you work with others toward shared goals.

- Schools often do not discuss inclusion openly, fearing that parents of disabled youngsters will feel short-changed about actual services for their child.

- Children and parents of children who have spent years in special education settings are bound to feel uncomfortable and to have problems adjusting to the general education curriculum, requirements and students.

- Parents of nondisabled students also have concerns because more academically and behaviorally needy students are in the classroom with students who are average or above average academically. You can be sure that parents of the highly motivated and academically successful are going to be vocal about their concerns for lowered standards and less help and instructional time for their children.

When talking with parents, you might want to start with recent reports indicating that a number of included students have done much better socially and academically. Legislators feel that special needs students perform at a higher level when offered precision teaching by general education subject "experts," support from special educators and the challenge of general education peers. Socially, many included students have reported they feel more part of school and more willing to involve themselves in school activities. Legislators point out that the dual system, prior to inclusion, resulted in dismal test scores as well as disappointing graduation rates for the disabled. Moreover, many students referred to their special education classes as "happy" classes, where they didn't have an opportunity to study what their friends in general education were studying.

BRIGHT IDEA

Be certain you are prepared with accurate information about inclusion in your school before meeting with parents. Find out from your principal the school's policy on inclusion and how you are expected to discuss it. You need to know to what extent staff, parents, students and administration have been informed and are involved.

The better informed you are, the better prepared you are to help parents understand inclusion and, most importantly, to enlist their support in educating their child. Here are a few suggestions:

- Be ready to answer: How has the school staff prepared for inclusion?

- Be prepared with specifics: Where, when, by whom and with whom will special needs children be included?

(Has the Committee on Special Education incorporated education in an inclusion class in the IEP?)

- To what standards will special needs children who are included be held? What if the standards are not met?

- What type of supplemental or remedial help will be given? Where, by whom and how frequently will assistance be offered?

- How have parents and students been notified about inclusion?

Opening the lines of communication with parents or guardians

The beginning of the school year is jam packed with so many things for you to do that it is hard to focus on something not directly involved with your teaching responsibilities. Perhaps you feel that parental contact falls in the category of another chore, one pretty far down on the list of things you simply must do. This may well be one of those situations where "putting off until tomorrow what you can do today" does not serve you well.

"Write a simple personal note introducing you and your coteacher and inviting parents to become involved."

Consider devising a simple personal note introducing you and your coteacher and inviting parents to become involved. You can cite convenient contact times and phone numbers while explaining your need for their support. This is an ideal opportunity to include pertinent classroom standards regarding homework as well as basic academic and behavioral expectations. To better ensure that parents get your letter, count it as one of the first homework assignments. Explain to students that they will receive credit for it when it is returned with a parent's signature. Leave space for comments, questions and a signature as well as a place to write in the most convenient contact times and phone numbers for you to reach them.

bottom line
∎ ∎ ∎ ∎ ∎ ∎ ∎ ∎ ∎ ∎

Teachers can learn more from problems than from solutions.

Your first face-to-face parent conference

Before you know it, it will be time for the first of several scheduled parent-teacher conferences. From past experience, I have learned not to be surprised and not to make assumptions about who will be able to attend and why some will not. Increasingly, I have begun to appreciate the complexity of the lives of our parents or guardians and the effort made to meet us to hear our "words of wisdom."

Recent statistics show that a high percentage of students come from homes where both parents work, or from a home where one parent works two jobs. Parents share that they feel stressed and overwhelmed with the busyness of their schedules and want nothing more than some quiet time with nothing they "have to do." The truth is that parent-teacher conferences are among the items they feel tempted to scratch from their must-do list. When questioned, parents often remark that they have little or no opportunity at a conference to express how they feel and that they leave feeling it was unproductive. We somehow must make our conferences something that parents or guardians truly feel are important so that regular contact with the school and teachers will be on their must-do list.

"We must make parents feel conferences are important so that regular contact with the school will be on their must-do list."

Creating a positive climate for parent conferences

The following tips will help you maintain a strong and positive collaborative relationship with parents and guardians:

- Your school will have scheduled dates and times for you to have conferences, but do not feel limited by the minimal dates set aside for that purpose.

- Smile. Meet and greet each parent or guardian, demonstrating your pleasure in their attendance.

- Make sure you know their name as well as the correct pronunciation. Do you know the correct title and relationship to the student?

- Make the seating arrangement as pleasant and comfortable as possible. Preferably use a table with equal height chairs; if possible, sit on a diagonal to the parent or guardian to promote a feeling of cooperation and common purpose. Do not sit at your desk while offering them a student desk.

- Use language appropriate to the parent. Do not talk up or down or use educational jargon. If a language barrier exists,

bottom line
■ ■ ■ ■ ■ ■ ■ ■ ■ ■

"People who wait for all conditions to be perfect before acting, never act."— *John Capozzi* try to get a translator. Perhaps another staff member can help you out. At times, I have found a willing older student most helpful in this capacity. (If you use a translator, underscore the need for confidentiality.)

■ Keep the meeting focused. Have goals. Allow parental input in determining the topics to be covered. Recognize the value of parents' time. Have your curriculum outline, grade book and samples of their child's work handy. Tangible work samples will reinforce your comments.

■ Learn to listen; listen to learn. Real communication involves give and take. Make it obvious that you want to know the parents' concerns, ideas, suggestions and even their criticisms. Particularly ask, "What works well with _____? What have you found to be effective?" "What is it that _____ loves to do?" Let parents talk, and jot down some of their ideas.

■ Share information about their child. Work as a team to solve problems. Be as positive as possible, pointing out specific academic or behavioral traits they can feel pleased about. If there are problem areas, give examples showing how or why improvement is necessary. Discuss how, together, you might help the student effect changes.

■ Encourage parents or guardians to stay in contact, whether by note, phone call, visit or email (if that works for you). Prepare a handout with your contact information, convenient times and appropriate phone numbers.

BRIGHT IDEA

Bear in mind that many parents or guardians of special needs students are exasperated, depressed, confused and frustrated by the label or disability. Negative school reports and critical remarks may have made them cautious and even angry with their children and teachers. Consider what you say and how you say it. Repeated negative phone calls, notes and comments may exacerbate the situation or even result in child abuse or counterproductive disciplinary action.

For most productive results from parents and students, focus on student strengths whenever possible. Attempt to collaborate to overcome specific student deficiencies and specific problem behaviors.

■ Keep a parent contact log. Date it. Jot down special tips, hints and suggestions. Use this log at every contact to help you with record keeping and follow-up. This can be especially important when you have a difficult issue to discuss with the parent or guardian. When phoning home, perhaps say "Hello, I'm glad I caught you at home. I need your support about _____."

■ Thank parents or guardians for their attendance and support.

Developing and maintaining relationships with parents or guardians

Once parents or guardians have met you and begin to trust that you are sincerely eager to help them help their child, your chances for an ongoing relationship are increased immeasurably. Because many of our students live in a blended family environment, it is critical to be alert to the sensitive issues stepparents face. Your goal must be to demonstrate your continuing concern for the child and parent and to maximize the effects of each contact.

■ Prepare for phone or personal conferences by gathering specific information and materials that will be helpful in furthering the purpose of your conference.

■ Make every effort to meet the time constraints of working parents, perhaps meeting briefly before school or during the school day in a planning or lunch period. Try to be flexible to accommodate their schedules.

■ Prepare a handout of suggestions on how parents can help their child at home. Include some potential online resources. Distribute to those parents who indicate interest. (See supplemental materials at the end of this chapter.)

■ Prepare a handout of tips for recognizing a student at risk for academic or behavior problems, with suggestions on how to help and how to develop a mutually reinforcing home-school discipline plan. Distribute to interested parents.

"Once parents begin to trust that you are eager to help them help their child, your chances for an ongoing relationship are increased."

bottom line
■ ■ ■ ■ ■ ■ ■ ■ ■ ■

All children can learn! "Nothing is so powerful as an idea whose time has come!"—*Victor Hugo*

- Prepare copies of school and community resources for student and parent support. Distribute to interested parents.

- Suggest that the PTA and administration collaborate on parenting skills presentations throughout the year.

- Consider developing a mentoring program. Think of the gifts that parents or grandparents can bring to the education of children. Parents can be ideal resources for helping special needs children. Also, parents and even grandparents may have specialized information to share as classroom guest speakers for teachers. (This needs to be cleared through your school administration prior to implementation.)

BRIGHT IDEA

Forge a positive relationship with parents or guardians by signaling, verbally and nonverbally, your respect for them and their child. Offer your assistance in working with their child. Ask the following:

- How can I help you?
- How can I help your child?
- What special information about your child should I know?
- When, where and how can I contact you?

Always convey a willingness to work with parents. Parents have special information to contribute that can be beneficial to mutual goals for their child. Make parents comfortable by signaling receptiveness to their techniques, strategies, successes and failures.

Working with foster parents

I'm sure you have noticed that some of our students do not live in traditional family units, A very special group of people exist in our community who are willing to embrace other people's children—children who have been abandoned, neglected and abused. These special people become foster parents and often face enormous challenges in their efforts to overcome the effects of abuse, neglect and grief on their foster children. Raising our own well-loved children is no easy task; the job of foster parents can be staggering.

Bear in mind that teachers and schools need to be aware of the legal guardianship of students and maintain accurate records to ensure the confidentiality of information and the safety of students.

- Foster children often develop special strategies for survival. It takes a special person a long time to break down the defensive wall that many of these children have built as a barrier. Compassionate teachers will recognize that foster parents need reassurance and understanding when faced with their foster child's truancy, lying and disruptiveness—behaviors sometimes used by foster children to capture attention, seek revenge or avoid failure.

FYI

More than half a million children are receiving foster care services; children of color and urban children are overrepresented. Many have been cycled through multiple homes and have a history of abuse and rejection. Foster parents may receive little or no assistance in parenting these neglected and troubled children. (Schwartz, 1999; Stride, 2004)

- Foster children often feel little connection to school, class assignments or academic and behavioral expectations. For this reason, a special effort by teachers to provide ongoing support can be effective in keeping foster parents informed of assignments and progress when their foster children fail to do so.

- Extra sensitivity in soliciting information and giving advice goes a long way in avoiding a perception by foster parents of intrusiveness. Many state and federal agencies hold them accountable. They may resent their foster child's teacher and school also intruding, especially if they have no personal relationship with them.

Our schools in the United States have changed radically over the past few decades. Newspapers and TV programs remind us that the American face is changing. Some research indicates that one out of three Americans is African-American, Hispanic, Asian American, American Indian or of mixed ancestry. This significant change has impacted our schools greatly, often involving treatment and placement issues. New federal legislation, the No Child Left Behind (NCLB) legislation, underscores a deep concern regarding

bottom line
■ ■ ■ ■ ■ ■ ■ ■ ■ ■

"The foundation of any state is the education of its youth."—*Diogenes* significant disparities in the identification and placement of minorities in special education programs.

There have been many uplifting stories about school staffs that have been successful in making tremendous progress educating our minority youth. Unfortunately, this success is not yet widespread. Breaking the negative cycle of minority underachievement is paramount in a country that treasures its children, treasures economic growth and treasures a strong democracy. It is essential that we use the best practices to ensure that all of our children learn. It must be a cooperative effort by parent, teacher and student.

FYI

The Department of Education has indicated that services provided to students with limited English proficiency often do not meet their needs and do not result in positive academic response. Further, the dropout rate is 68% higher for minorities than whites. (IDEA '97)

One challenge facing educators is better communication with our limited English speaking parents. In my district our early efforts were, at best, marginally successful. Through trial and error, we found that phone conversations or phone messages were ineffective. Perhaps there was (1) no phone, (2) a shared phone, (3) a parent or guardian working several jobs and unable to respond to calls or (4) an inability to understand English. Further, we found that fliers, newsletters, TV, radio or school websites were not informing these parents.

bottom line
■ ■ ■ ■ ■ ■ ■ ■ ■ ■

"A person's mind, stretched to a new idea, never goes back to its original dimension." [adapted]—*Oliver Wendell Holmes*

As we gathered information, we realized that we were caught up in our own little world and did not really make an effort to understand the plight of some of our parents. For some, getting time off from work during the day was not an easy feat, nor was getting the necessary transportation to the school. It was after Teresa Gomez came in to talk to me about her brother Juan that I really stopped to consider how much it meant to parents or guardians to help loved ones get a good education.

Perhaps 22 years of age, Teresa introduced herself in halting English and conveyed that she was Juan's guardian, his older sister. She was the sole supporter of her "inherited family" of four and had taken off from both of her jobs, ridden the bus and walked the rest of the way to make it in time for her conference. Although obviously very nervous, she told me that she was eager to help Juan at home but had little chance due to her work hours. Nonetheless, she indicated that she was very thankful for his opportunity and would encourage him to do his work. Although I speak rudimentary Spanish, there is no question that I felt frustration at my inability to really communicate with Teresa. My short time with her made me reflect on how I could improve my efforts to make real contact with parents and guardians.

Finally, it dawned on us to draw on the many resources available, ask our Hispanic coworkers and neighbors for suggestions and use the Internet as a tool. Practical experience, research and conversations with parents and friends of the limited English parents have shown that we might be able to increase the involvement of this critical group. Following are some of the ways that have been found helpful in removing barriers and encouraging the involvement of non–English speaking parents in home-school collaboration:

Two principal factors are involved in the barriers separating Hispanic parents and schools:

- Many low-income parents do not feel the right to question educators. Administrators and educators may mistake parental reserve for noninterest, thereby creating a cycle of mutual misunderstanding and, perhaps, distrust.

- Schools send out confusing signals. Often communication is not in the native language. Meetings are established at locations and times when parents or guardians are working. Further, too little effort is made to understand and meet the parents' needs. With few Hispanic educators to give guidance, there is little understanding of how to reach out to this vital parental resource. (Stride, 2004; Inger, 1992)

- Make it easy for parents and family members to attend and participate. Provide childcare (perhaps a student might volunteer to babysit for extra credit), translators (perhaps a student or bilingual staff member) and transportation, if necessary (perhaps another parent or social service staff member). Be sensitive to time and location needs.

bottom line
■ ■ ■ ■ ■ ■ ■ ■ ■ ■

Sensitivity to divergent cultures demands an understanding of verbal and nonverbal language, behavior and values.

- Attempt to make the meeting nonthreatening and informal. A welcoming smile and friendly social conversation are important.

- Focus on positive student behaviors and aspects of academic work. Try to convey a need for collaboration in overcoming specific deficiencies. If possible, offer simple tips for what parents could do.

BRIGHT IDEA

Consider using school social service staff proficient in the native language of parents or guardians to make home visits. Research on school-parent collaboration projects has shown that the most successful approach with Hispanic parents or guardians is personal. Face-to-face conversations in the native language seem most effective.

- Respond to the needs and concerns of parents at each meeting. Do not focus solely on your own agenda.

- Tap into your school's outreach program or encourage your school to develop an outreach program that can amplify your classroom efforts.

- Be alert to school or community programs that provide free vocational skill building courses as well as English language courses geared to limited English residents.

No Child Left Behind legislation

bottom line

■ ■ ■ ■ ■ ■ ■ ■ ■ ■

"Our dreams can come true—if we have the courage to pursue them."—
Walt Disney

The importance of parental involvement cannot be overemphasized in this global society, especially with an educational environment mandating higher standards for all. Let's talk in realistic terms about some teacher-parent opportunities. You probably have seen a lot about the NCLB legislation in the papers or on TV. (May I suggest a visit to the federal education website http://www.ed.gov/programs/) Perhaps you tuned out, assuming that NCLB was propaganda that would have no effect on your teaching. Contrarily, there are some important aspects of NCLB related to parents that you should be aware of. The way NCLB is written impacts on parents, teachers, school districts and the state, all in an effort to improve the educational opportunities for even the most needy of students. Let's take a look at how one section of the legislation might be important to you.

Key points in NCLB for parents

For schools or districts receiving federal funds from NCLB, certain requirements must be met, documented and reported:

LEGAL ALERT

The underlying purpose of NCLB legislation is to ensure that *all* children have a fair, equal opportunity to receive a high quality education that is academically challenging. Special provisions have been written into law focusing on low achieving and low performing children— the potential school dropouts. Additionally, recognizing the importance of shared parent-school responsibility for education, a section of the NCLB spells out procedures that should be implemented by schools or districts to encourage consultation and participation of parents.

If parents have questions about what is going on at school, what the curriculum is about and what are the standards for their child, NCLB offers help.

■ There must be a written parental involvement policy. (Does your school or district have one and have you read it?)

■ It must be written in language parents readily understand. (If your school population is predominately Hispanic, is the policy available in Spanish?)

■ The policy must describe how the school or district will involve parents in a timely and ongoing manner in the planning, review and improvement of programs related to curriculum, formal academic assessment procedures and the proficiency level students are expected to meet.

■ The joint responsibility of academic achievement, shared by parents, staff and students, must be clearly defined. (How has your school or district defined those responsibilities?)

bottom line
■ ■ ■ ■ ■ ■ ■ ■ ■ ■

"There is no security on this earth, only opportunity."— *General Douglas MacArthur*

FYI

Research shows a direct and positive relationship between parental involvement and student achievement. This relationship is enhanced when parents provide an environment for learning, communicate reasonably high standards and involve themselves in school and community. Parents can be assisted in this effort through access to Internet resources. Websites are available that focus on homework help, parenting guidance, parent-child activities, guidelines for safe-child Internet use and a wide variety of home-school activities and materials. (Yeok-Hwa & Ngeow, 1999; Stride, 2004)

No, you as a teacher are certainly not responsible for meeting these requirements, but it surely would be to your benefit to be advised of your district policies.

What does NCLB suggest to you, the busy classroom teacher? It shows unequivocally that the federal government is finally writing into legislation some of the things that you and I have long known and been talking about. Teachers cannot be everything to their students, know everything about their students or be totally responsible for their success or failure. We need parental help, input, support and guidance. We need informed parents, and as difficult as it may be initially to involve parents, the payoff will be huge in the long run.

Power of ◉ne

The Challenge

Mrs. Stennis, Eduardo's first grade teacher, was delighted to see that Eduardo's mother had come to the conference. Eduardo had been very upset earlier that morning, reporting that his mother was at work picking tomatoes and couldn't get off from her job to come see his teacher. He was so proud of his mother and wanted Mrs. Stennis to meet her.

Mrs. Stennis warmed immediately to the broad smile and firm handshake Mrs. Ramirez shared. In simple English she spoke of her family's pride in their new Habitat for Humanity home—their first real home—and their determination that Eduardo and his younger sister finish school and not be "field hands," as she and her husband were. "He needs to be a good reader. It is muy importante. How can I help him? I can only read a little English."

The Response

Mrs. Stennis knew that this proud lady was sincere in her desire to help.

"What could be better, Mrs. Ramirez, than you reading with him? You will have time together, and you both will learn to read better. Look at these books here and pick out a few that you will be comfortable reading. You can return them at the end of the week and get others."

"How should I do it?" Mrs. Ramirez asked.

"Every night, have Eduardo pick a book. Together, you might first look through it at the pictures and guess what it is about. Then you read it first, but not too fast. After you read it, talk about the story. Then, perhaps you could have Eduardo try reading it to you. Both of you can take turns reading the book until you have mastered all the words. When Eduardo feels comfortable reading it, ask him to read it to his little sister. And sometime, when your schedule permits, wouldn't it be fun if you all went to the library and got library cards together? The librarian could help you select books, and then you could get whatever you like, perhaps even audio books."

HOW HOME AND SCHOOL
CAN WORK TOGETHER

Family-school collaboration strengthens the school experience. Students who know that parents and school staff are working together are less likely to cause problems and more likely to get appropriate and timely assistance should problems arise.

Ways to reinforce positive behavior at home and school

1. Obtain and read a copy of the school behavior code with your child. Obtain and read a copy of the teacher's classroom rules. Discuss with your child the rules and the consequences of infractions.

2. Work with your child to establish home rules aligned with the school rules. Keep them short, simple and easily enforced.

3. Be consistent and fair. Give immediate consequences, preferably after discussion with your child.

4. Promote your child's independence and responsibility by encouraging involvement in making rules and determining consequences.

5. Maintain your sense of humor.

6. Listen to your child's complaints and suggestions. Be objective in discussing them. Try to act on those with merit.

7. If there is a difficulty at school, first collect information from your child. Then, call the adult involved and listen to the school view. Attempt to reinforce the school code. Try not to bad-mouth the school or teacher. Most children immediately sense disharmony and use it to undermine a unified discipline effort.

8. If you disagree with the school consequence, arrange a conference to discuss your views in an objective manner. Be specific. Be open to alternative views.

9. If you have serious concerns about the disciplinary environment in the school, arrange to visit for a day. Note your concerns prior to scheduling a meeting with the appropriate school personnel.

10. Keep the focus on your child's safety and development of positive social behavior.

HOW TO HELP YOUR CHILD STUDY

Parents or guardians are invaluable in encouraging and supporting their child's academic growth. The following tips have been found to enhance study effectiveness and improve student success:

1. Encourage your child to use an assignment pad or calendar for writing homework assignments for each class. Check it nightly (or as needed).

2. Encourage your child to keep a notebook organized by subject area.

3. Check with the teacher to find out what the homework policy is.

4. Arrange a regular time to read, study and do homework assignments.

5. Establish a study spot—a quiet place at a table or desk with good light.

6. Have materials available (pen, pencil, ruler, compass, calculator, dictionary, computer if possible). Have a convenient storage area for work in progress or resources (could be as simple as a box).

7. Establish that homework time is a distraction-free time—no TV, phone calls, games, loud music, etc.

8. Be available for help or discussion. Show an interest in assignments and class work. Try to discuss school subjects during the normal course of conversation.

9. Be a good role model. Read or do quiet work while your child studies or does homework.

10. Discuss the instructions for assignments to ascertain that your child will be on target. Monitor work toward completion of assignments.

11. Contact the teacher if your child is having difficulty completing assignments or if the work seems too hard or too easy.

12. Check long-range assignments; monitor progress. Help your child establish goals and intermediate steps.

13. Make a habit of regular library use for research and pleasure reading.

14. Discuss how to improve study habits. Encourage a nightly review of notes and assignments. Ask your child if you can give an oral quiz.

15. Use the television as a learning tool. Check listings for programs that will enhance studies.

16. Review procedures for making up missing assignments due to absence from class.

17. Give lots of encouragement.

18. Give lots of praise whenever appropriate.

WARNING SIGNS OF ACADEMIC FAILURE

As the school year progresses, you may notice some early warning signs that a problem is developing. They may help you decide whether your child may be at risk for failure. Be alert. Be supportive. Be ready to intervene. Be certain to contact your child's teacher regarding your specific concerns. Warning signs include the following:

1. Generalized depressed attitude.

2. Lack of interest and involvement in school courses or activities.

3. Poor or failing test grades or class work grades.

4. No papers brought home; books or homework not shared with you.

5. Refusal to share information about classes and grades; annoyance when asked.

6. School reports of behavior problems involving your child.

7. Difficulty focusing on written or reading assignments.

8. Does not seem to study or know how to study for exams.

9. Bored—claims subject matter is too difficult and will never master it, or claims already knows it.

10. Little attempt to do homework or study regularly; does not carry books or notebooks to and from school.

Your child may demonstrate several of the above behaviors and not be at-risk for academic failure. But you know your child better than most. If the signs are recurring and pervasive, your child may have a problem that you need to address ASAP!

INTERNET RESOURCES FOR PARENTS

Ample research underscores the high correlation between parental involvement and student achievement. The Internet is a quick, efficient and inexpensive method of accessing parenting resources to support home-school learning. If you do not have a computer, your public library probably has computers for your use as well as someone to help you learn how to use the Internet. The following sites are suggested by the National Parent Information Network:

Parents Guide to the Internet
http://www.ed.gov/pubs/parents/internet/index.html

The Children's Partnership: Overview
http://www.childrenspartnership.org/bbar/ctech.html

TEAMS Educational Resources
http://teams.lacoe.edu/

The National Parent Information Network
http://npin.org/

Family Involvement in Children's Education: Successful Local Approaches
http://www.ed.gov/pubs/ [Search *family involvement*]

North Central Regional Educational Laboratory
Parent Involvement: Literature Review and Database of Promising Practices
http://www.ncrel.org/sdrs/pidata/pi0over.htm

SafeKids.Com
Child Safety on the Information Highway
http://www.safekids.com/child_safety.htm

Family TLC
Family parenting tips, activities, articles on child development.
http://familyTLC.net

Kids Can Learn!
http://www.kidscanlearn.com/

Dealing With Tough Issues Series: QuickTips® for Parents
http://www.parent-institute.com

Helping Your Child With Homework
http://www.ed.gov/pubs/ [Search *homework help*]

Parenting TIPS: Timely Intervention Parental Strategies
http://www.drjunestride.com

ESTABLISHING A CLIMATE FOR PRODUCTIVE PARENT-TEACHER CONFERENCES

A few minutes preparation before a conference will go a long way in building a collaborative relationship that will help students, parents and you. How prepared are you?

Yes No

☐ ☐ 1. Do you know the correct relationship of the student and the adult you are meeting (parent, stepparent, foster parent, relative, guardian)?

☐ ☐ 2. Are you prepared to greet them with their correct name and title?

☐ ☐ 3. Is the person legally responsible for the student? If not, what is your school policy about sharing information?

☐ ☐ 4. Do you speak the primary language of the parent or guardian? If not, do you have a translator available?

☐ ☐ 5. If the parent has to bring children, do you have a place for them to sit, work or play?

☐ ☐ 6. Do you have available current samples of the student's work, tests and projects, as well as your grade book?

☐ ☐ 7. Can you make at least two positive statements about the student (e.g., about academic work, motivation, participation, cooperation, behavior)?

☐ ☐ 8. Have you established uninterrupted time for the conference?

☐ ☐ 9. Do you have a comfortable, quiet and fairly private location (i.e., appropriate size chair, table for both of you in the back of your room)?

☐ ☐ 10. Are you ready to greet them with a smile?

☐ ☐ 11. Have you some questions to ask them about ways you can work more effectively with their child?

☐ ☐ 12. Do you have a notebook or log to jot down helpful information, contact addresses and phone numbers?

☐ ☐ 13. Do you have specific suggestions about how the parent or guardian can support academic growth or positive behavior?

☐ ☐ 14. Are you ready and willing to listen openly to their concerns, needs and critical comments?

☐ ☐ 15. Do you have a follow-up plan to ensure ongoing collaboration?

☐ ☐ 16. Are you prepared to thank them for their attendance?

Preparing for Inclusion

THE KEYS

Bob Cassidy woke up in a cold sweat, deeply perplexed. For the past five nights he had been haunted by dreams. Each night the dream started out the same; each night the dream concluded differently and disturbingly. In his dreams Bob saw a teacher, who resembled himself, drive to Spring Street Elementary School and park in the side parking area. He looked anxious and a bit confused. He exited his car in a purposeful manner and strode toward the front of the school.

Night 1 The teacher walked up the pathway and entered the school through the main door. He walked down a hallway and came to Classroom 14; he tried the door. The door was locked. Confused, he shrugged his shoulders, turned and walked away.

Night 2 The teacher walked up the pathway and entered the school through the main door. He walked down a hallway and came to Classroom 14; he tried the door. The door was locked. He thought a moment and wandered off to find someone to open the door. No one was available. Perplexed, he shook his head and walked away.

"Establish yourself as a friendly, essential and supportive presence in the school."

Night 3 The teacher walked up the pathway and entered the school through the main door. He walked down a hallway and came to Classroom 14, a key in hand. He tried the key in the lock but it did not fit. The door still would not open. Exasperated, he sighed and walked away.

Night 4 The teacher walked up the pathway and entered the school through the main door. He walked down a hallway and came to Classroom 14, a key ring with several keys in his hand. One by one, he tried each key. None of them opened the door. Annoyed, he walked away.

Night 5 The teacher walked up the pathway and entered the school through the main door. He walked down a hallway past Classroom 14, a key ring with several keys in his hand. He stopped at Classroom 15, selected a key and inserted it into the lock. The door opened. Surprised and relieved, he smiled and walked into Classroom 15.

What do the dreams mean to Bob Cassidy? Were they somehow a portent of his upcoming school year? Did they have a significance for the new year, his first teaching an inclusion class? Bob spent a lot of time speculating about what the dreams might be conveying. And what about you? Are your end-of-summer, back-to-school dreams ones that comfort and refresh or provoke and puzzle you as you reflect about the challenges you will be facing in your inclusion setting? Moreover, how can you best prepare?

bottom line
■ ■ ■ ■ ■ ■ ■ ■ ■ ■

It is not the cards you are dealt but how you play them that counts.—
Anonymous

Most teachers, particularly those venturing into the inclusion world, find that the concluding weeks of summer vacation are filled with speculation and perhaps a good measure of apprehension. Questions keep surfacing for which they probably have few or no answers: What and how many students will be in the class? How many students will be identified as those with special needs? What role will I play on the inclusion team? Will I be a working with other professionals, paraprofessionals or a consultant teacher?

What role will I play on the inclusion team? How will we work together? How will our teaching styles mesh?

Bob Cassidy was convinced that his dreams conveyed the importance of preparation, flexibility and tenacity. The teacher in the dreams did not stop trying. When one option proved unsuccessful, he tried another. When he realized that all the options he had tried for Classroom 14 would not unlock the door, he reflected, reprocessed and made a decision to try something totally new—Classroom 15. It was then that the key fit, the door opened and Bob walked in only to find other challenges. You, too, may find yourself looking for the key to unlock new challenges as well. You may find that former keys (strategies, remedies and options) are not giving the expected results. You may feel frustration, annoyance and confusion in the process of experimentation, as options and opportunities unfold. Be patient with yourself. Growth rarely is easy. Growth necessitates change. Positive professional growth requires persistence, flexibility and, certainly, a willing heart and mind.

This chapter will indirectly respond to Bob Cassidy's dreams. It will also offer insight into how to set the tone for students, for yourself, for collaborating colleagues and for a successful beginning to the year through purposeful preparation. What preparations can you make for that important first day?

You are on the pathway to an inclusion adventure. You will encounter many variables along the way, some known and others unknown. By being prepared, you can identify and address certain variables. Others will present more of a challenge.

This chapter is designed to eliminate potential obstacles that could deter progress with your students. Preparation is key to maximizing your time and effort. The better prepared you are, the less chance for you to lose direction and momentum.

bottom line
■ ■ ■ ■ ■ ■ ■ ■ ■ ■

The Chinese symbol for adversity contains the symbol for opportunity.

The five Ps discussed in this chapter—personnel, physical needs, paperwork, procedures, PR—are keys you can use before you get immersed in school. They each require reflection, research and a positive attitude.

Key 1: Personnel preparation

Network. Network. Network. Think of it as a mantra. Inclusion demands teamwork for success. The more resources you have that are part of your inclusion effort, the greater the chances of help when support is needed. Teachers in elementary schools often remark how much they love the opportunity to make a difference shaping the lives of children but complain that they feel *so all alone*. In particular, specialists often feel segregated from the school community and claim that many teachers don't know who they are, what they do or how they can assist.

Sandy Connelly asked a question often repeated by specialists in elementary schools. (Indeed many general educators have shared a similar concern.) "How can I feel more a part of the school teaching team? I want to work with my colleagues and be a part of the whole school effort." Sandy, our itinerant speech teacher, had a schedule that made getting to know and collaborate with other teachers next to impossible. Sandy was assigned to Spring Street Elementary School to give individualized instruction to identified students. She was scheduled to arrive after the beginning of the school day and to leave prior to the end of the day. Yes, on paper, she was part of the inclusion team, but emotionally and practically, she was doing her own thing with little collaboration, no support and no professional sharing. Colleagues teasingly called her the ghost of Spring Street Elementary. Sandy laughed with them but inside she found it anything but funny. Not only did she feel isolated from her peers, she also felt that her work engendered negative feelings for herself and for the students she was assigned to assist.

This is no small thing, especially for teachers striving to grow professionally. Sharing techniques, materials and new ideas as well as brainstorming solutions to problems should be a part of every teacher's life, especially for those involved in inclusion. Sometimes it takes finesse to make certain that collaboration can be built into a schedule. Also, I would suggest that you consider how best to be *proactive*. You will have to be your own ambassador, meeting and greeting administrators, colleagues and students at every opportunity.

bottom line
■ ■ ■ ■ ■ ■ ■ ■ ■ ■

Never doubt that a small group of thoughtful committed citizens [teachers] can change the world. Indeed, it's the only thing that ever has.—
Margaret Mead

If few opportunities occur naturally, you will have to create some! Make people glad to see you and impress them with your willingness to help. Establish yourself as a friendly, essential and supportive presence in the school—with administrators, teachers and, most importantly, students.

The following are some tried and true methods that teachers have found effective, even by those special teachers assigned to several schools or classrooms.

"Use your digital camera to make a directory of key people in school that you can share with your students."

1. Make your own '"Who's Who in Our School" booklet. Get to know staff by name even before they know you! Make it a special project to cheerfully greet the custodians, secretaries, nurses, cafeteria staff, librarians, gym teachers, counselors, special teachers and, of course, the regular staff of administrators and teachers. Go out of your way to exchange some pleasantry and to share a positive comment. Consider using your digital camera to make your own directory of key people in school that you can share with your students while refreshing your own memory).

2. Seek out those professionals and staff members who always demonstrate a willingness to assist students and teachers, those people who are positive, flexible lovers of children. Surround yourself by positive people. Keep a talent file to help you remember the special abilities of staff who could possibly mentor students. Mentors often bond in ways that resonate with special needs students. Remember mentors do not have to be teachers; they do have to be positive role models as well as lovers of children.

bottom line
■ ■ ■ ■ ■ ■ ■ ■ ■ ■

I am only one, but I am still one. I cannot do everything, but still I can do something. And because I cannot do everything I will not refuse to do the something that I can do.—*Helen Keller*

3. Let your enthusiasm leak out! Convey your professionalism (and humor) in your attitude, conversation and demeanor. Smiles are contagious. Share yours with staff and students. Students and teachers in inclusion classes need all the positive PR and support they can get. Caution: Retain the privacy and status of all special needs students!

4. Offer your talents and time to others. Make every effort to find out the needs of colleagues and support them whenever and however you can.

5. Establish your reliability. Be on time; better yet, be early. Be prepared. Do more than requested. Building trust is essential to establishing your network. Take time to give credit to others and to communicate their successes.

It is tempting to set high expectations for others but not for yourself. Unfortunately, some teachers do the least amount they can get away with and somehow manage to claim credit for the good works of others. Obviously this is not the way to win friends, influence people positively and establish a network of professionals eager to collaborate with you!

Key 2: Physical preparation

No, I am not talking about your personal exercise plan here, although that is certainly something I would highly recommend for reducing stress. I am referring to the classroom environment—the physical space that you, your collaborator and your students will be sharing. Think about it; when you go into a dreary, disorganized and dirty space, don't you just want to escape? Rooms that are airy, organized, clean and cheerful invite you to stay. They issue a nonverbal welcome that is much needed by all, especially those students who are particularly nervous about acceptance.

Your inclusion class will have spatial needs that a noninclusion class might not. Here are a few things to consider:

1. Tables and desks should be placed for ease of movement to allow for independent work that requires privacy as well as small group or partner work that requires sharing materials and ideas. Structure a quiet area for reading or research. Importantly, leave space so that collaborating teachers are able to circulate throughout the work areas to support and oversee student work.

This is a fine opportunity to demonstrate your consideration and appreciation of your collaborator. You can imagine the hurt and embarrassment one of my colleagues felt when it became obvious that she was too large to fit between the desks to assist students. Not unexpectedly, a few of the students felt compelled to

bottom line
∎ ∎ ∎ ∎ ∎ ∎ ∎ ∎ ∎ ∎

Real integrity is doing the right thing, knowing that nobody's going to know whether you did it or not.—
Oprah Winfrey

make jokes about her size, snickering under their breath that "Big Momma can't fit; Big Momma's in a snit."

2. A work area and storage area should be cleared and set aside for collaborator's supplies, materials and personal belongings.

3. Furniture should allow for unobstructed views of the chalkboard and AV equipment.

4. Ready access to everyday texts and supplies as well as research materials will make it easier to individualize student lessons to accommodate special needs.

5. Determine a clearly visible location for computers and AV equipment. Ascertain that computers and all AV equipment are in good mechanical order. They will play an essential part in teaching multimodal lessons to satisfy the needs of the more able and more disabled in your class.

6. You will need a locked file cabinet or closet for securing IEPs and other legal documents.

7. Make a plea for up-to-date computers and software with voice recognition, microphones and headphones. Have a technologically handy friend hook up one computer for large screen demonstrations and research.

8. Select a clearly visible location for posting daily homework assignments. Make it understood that homework assignments would always be posted in that particular location.

9. Consider constructing a chart or graph for students to check their personal record of completed and missing assignments.

10. Use the bulletin board as a tool and teaching assistant. Post your classroom rules in simple and positive short sentences. Consider using a digital camera to make an easy "getting to know you" display of photos and names of teachers and students in the class. The display can be augmented later to include comments about each student's hobbies and special interests.

bottom line
■ ■ ■ ■ ■ ■ ■ ■ ■ ■

Give me a fruitful error anytime, full of seeds, bursting with its own corrections.—
Vilfredo Pareto

BRIGHT IDEA

Students with special needs who are new to the inclusion setting may be accustomed to a more structured environment and schedule than are students in general education classes. Moreover, the added stimulus in general education may require some behavioral adjustment on the part of the newly included. Designate an area in the room for timeout for students (not just students with special needs!) who are out of control and need to sit quietly before rejoining a class activity. Do not make timeout seem punitive; rather suggest that at times we all need an opportunity to regain calmness and focus.

Most importantly, you and your collaborator have to make a philosophical decision: Will the room be set up so that teaching is student-centered or teacher-centered? The answer to that question will help determine the placement and use of teacher desks in relation to student desks and other materials and supplies. Oftentimes, new teachers work to establish student rapport and effectiveness in management prior to implementing a student-centered approach.

Key 3: Paperwork preparation

I heard that moan! Indeed, I often lamented the time spent on what I felt to be useless paperwork. Paperwork is often considered one of the most dreaded aspects of teaching, especially if it is considered of little value and reduces available time for things deemed more important. On the flip side some paperwork may allow you to work smarter and more effectively.

Be proactive in securing administrative guidelines and expectations. Your time spent here can be your safety net for the year! For example:

1. Check your teacher handbook for the policies on student attendance, daily attendance reports, discipline, dress codes, passing/failing grades, initiating parental contact, and reporting suspected abuse or physical/emotional problems. If the answers are not set forth clearly, ask

for a conference with your immediate supervisor to secure the answers.

2. What is the requirement regarding lesson plans, especially for collaborating teachers?

3. In what manner and how often will you both be evaluated? When will you be observed and what will be the criteria for determining your success? (Do not be hesitant to ask. Put your supervisors on notice that you are a professional who intends to be successful.)

4. Do you have the IEPs for your students with special needs? Are there BIPs for any of your students? Are you expected to disseminate copies of IEPs and BIPs to any other staff members?

5. Do you have a copy of school or district policy on inclusion that has been shared with staff, parents or students? Are you prepared to discuss any concerns with administrators? Are you prepared to convey the policy to parents and students?

Federal and state regulations must be followed in regard to suspected child abuse. Ascertain that the school policy spells out exactly what you must do and whom you must contact. Further, for your own protection, never transport a student in your own vehicle.

6. Importantly, what has your school or district scheduled for professional development regarding inclusion? What resources are available (e.g., books, videos, personal resources)? Is staff development money available for you and your collaborator to attend workshops or seminars on inclusion?

7. Do you have the schedules of special instructors who will be working with one or more of your special needs students? Do they have any schedule flexibility? It may be very helpful to you to offer preferred times and methods for their work with the students (perhaps you could offer two preferred times that work best).

Key 4: Procedural preparation

Dahlia has a severe neurological and muscular disorder that confines her to a wheelchair. She has a paraprofessional assigned to take her to the bathroom, lunch and all other school commitments. Her IEP specifies that in case of emergency (bomb scare, fire) she must be escorted to a predetermined location known by administration and emergency services for rescue purposes. As our schools include more students with severe disabilities, it behooves teachers to prepare for such emergencies.

BRIGHT IDEA

Be certain that paraprofessionals know the predetermined emergency plans and that such information is also readily available for substitute teachers.

Waiting until the need arises to think through procedures often confounds what already might be a stressful situation. The following are some situations for which to prepare:

1. Exactly what is expected of you in case of emergency in your room? Are you to send a student to get a hall guard? Are you to use an intercom system to make a distress call? Is the procedure clear to you? Is it a procedure you feel comfortable following?

   One year a young student in a neighboring class fell to the floor with a grand mal seizure. The other students had been in class with her the previous year and seemed to know instinctively to stay clear and immediately notify an authority figure. The school procedure for such a medical emergency was to use the intercom to immediately call the health office for assistance. The teacher attempted to do just that but, unfortunately, had not checked to see if the intercom key enabled her to make the call. It did not. The teacher was put in the difficult situation of trying to determine how best to get immediate help. She decided not to waste time with the intercom and sent a responsible student for help.

2. Do you know the exit route for fire or evacuation drills? Do you have any students with special needs who require

bottom line

It's not whether you get knocked down; it's whether you get back up.—
Vince Lombardi

assistance? What is expected in case of a bomb threat or terrorist attack? Of course we don't want to think that such information will ever be needed, but better to be prepared than panicked.

Federal and state legislation mandates that districts or schools provide for professional development of staff. Districts must budget money and submit official reports that show staff involvement in professional development. Make your needs and wishes known. The more specific your requests, the better the chances of having them fulfilled. Further, your sincere interest in becoming a more skilled professional will be noted!

3. What is the school policy regarding discipline? clothing? suspected child abuse? suspected drug abuse? dispensing medical prescriptions to students? Who is your immediate contact person? Is there paperwork involved? What must you do to be in compliance with school, district, state and federal rules? Make certain your class rules and expectations are in harmony with those of the school.

4. How should you handle parental contact? We had several principals in a short time and jokingly referred to the administrative handbook as that book of fast changing rules. We were never quite sure what the current principal's procedures were. One principal wanted regular parent contact by phone and notes and really encouraged parent visitations. Another had a different attitude. He expected to preapprove all letters or notes that were to go home. No one who was not signed in by office staff and issued an official pass was admitted to the school or any classroom. A third principal insisted that a phone log be kept, indicating to whom we spoke, date, time and substance of the call. Further, for legal reasons, two teachers were expected to share the room during any out-of-class contact with a student, parent or guardian.

5. What does your administration suggest in regard to daily concerns such as allowing students out of the classroom to go to the bathroom, get a drink of water, go to the nurse or make a phone call? Are students permitted in the hall unaccompanied? Are there regulation school passes? Can you develop your own system of passes? Does your

bottom line
■ ■ ■ ■ ■ ■ ■ ■ ■ ■

If you don't like the way something looks, then look at it differently.—
George Kelly

classroom door need to be locked from the outside at all times?

6. Keeping accurate attendance records is a legal requirement. In case of emergency evacuation, be certain to bring your attendance register with you. What do you as the classroom teacher have to do? Are any special duties or reports required of inclusion teachers? Do you send notification by computer to an attendance office? Are daily attendance forms picked up from your room and delivered to a central location? Do you keep a written attendance record that indicates the reason for tardiness or absence?

7. What is the school policy on remedial help? Is there a breakfast help club available? Is after school tutoring provided? What is the official stance on offering assistance after school on an individual basis? Think this through carefully. Too many teachers have learned the hard way about the consequences of working in a closed room without a colleague to oversee. No matter how noble or innocent your motives, a student charge of sexual abuse could spell the end of a professional career.

8. Finally, have you and your collaborator thought through classroom procedures that you expect students to follow for such things as homework, handing in materials, movement around class, extra help, and trips for water, to the bathroom or to the nurse? Do not expect your students to automatically know what to do. Make your expectations, as well as the consequences for noncompliance, clear to all students.

BRIGHT IDEA

Let technology lighten your load and enhance your effectiveness. Most parents now use email to keep in touch with loved ones. Ask permission from your supervisor to send a weekly communiqué to parents in which you offer encouragement and help, homework or special project assignments, and information about upcoming classroom study or events. This allows you to keep parents informed. Importantly, it gives parents or guardians a quick and simple manner of keeping in contact.

Key 5: PR preparation

Never underestimate the importance of your public relations, especially if you are eager to gain approval for students in your inclusion class as well as your inclusion work. (Caution: Use discretion by not identifying students with special needs.) When you positively and confidently convey the fine academic results of your students, the exciting projects that involve your students and the way inclusion is working in your classroom, you have a win-win situation. You win because your professionalism is respected and your inclusion successes inspire others. Students win because their good work and work habits are yielding positive results. The school and parents win because students are succeeding.

I strongly urge you to consider how to develop and implement a classroom PR program. Here are some simple ways you can advertise success:

1. Find out the district policy on websites. Can you regularly contribute to either the district or the school website? Establish and use a standard form for a weekly post of what's happening in your classroom. (Better yet, see if you have a technologically proficient student who can assist.) Include suggestions for better study habits, current or upcoming assignments, behavioral expectations, your contact information and so forth.

2. Ask parents or guardians for their email addresses. Send home a weekly communiqué by Internet or hard copy for students without email. Use the "Keep it simple, stupid"

LEGAL ALERT

No Child Left Behind requires all teachers to be "highly qualified" by 2005. The US Department of Education recently launched a new teacher-to-teacher professional development website with free online courses about research based practices and methods that have been successfully used in classrooms. Check with your administration to see if you are eligible to get in-service or continuing education credits by taking one of the courses. (www.paec.org/teacher2teacher)

Most of the Teacher-to-Teacher courses offered focus on English, Language Arts, Math and Science (e.g., Looking at Vocabulary, Reading in Content Areas: It's Just Different, Beginning to Write).

(KISS) principle. Always be positive. Give brief and helpful information about how parents can work with their child toward educational success.

3. Volunteer to be responsible for a hall bulletin board to showcase your class's fine work. Have a team of students "win" the special honor of developing the bulletin board.

4. Speak up at faculty or department meetings about positive academic or behavioral results to underscore success in inclusion collaboration. Give credit to collaborators and students. Remember the 4 Bs: Be brief, be positive, be humorous (if possible) and be seated.

5. Ask for the opportunity to make a brief presentation (or have students star in a brief presentation), sharing student successes at PTA or school board meetings.

6. Develop a monthly class newsletter, written and published by your students. Share samples of student work. Let the newsletter enhance your efforts to improve student writing and publishing skills.

7. Be your own ambassador whenever speaking with others. Share encouraging news about your inclusion class. Speak positively about your collaborators.

bottom line
■ ■ ■ ■ ■ ■ ■ ■ ■ ■

Each day comes bearing its own gifts. Untie the ribbons.—
Ruth Ann Schabacker

8. Nothing is ever going to be perfect, but look for the good. Expect the best.

I hope the five *P* keys will provide you with a safety net that allows you and your collaborator to work confidently and devote your time and energy to the needs of all your students.

Power of (●)ne

The Challenge

Spring Street Elementary School had no official novice teacher mentoring program since the grant money ran out. New teachers attended a two-day "welcome to our district" seminar and received a new teacher packet, a pep talk and a key to their room. From that time forward, the laissez-faire attitude resembled the sink or swim approach. Regretfully, too many new teachers, overwhelmed with unwritten expectations, sunk. Georgiana Bishop was a brand new teacher who realized that panic was threatening to paralyze her thinking about what to do and how to do it. She needed informed help to get started on the right foot, and she needed it fast. But, she asked herself, where to turn?

The Response

To her credit, Georgiana had learned that hard work, coupled with willingness to admit the need for help, often enabled her to overcome obstacles that seemed insurmountable. She browsed through the staff directory she had received in her new teacher packet and scrolled down the short list of inclusion teachers, noting that one was the very person she had been told was a superb teacher. Almost immediately she made up her mind. She picked up the phone and called Ms. Jackson, a third grade inclusion teacher. Georgiana introduced herself, spent a few moments describing her panic and plight, and then invited Ms. Jackson for lunch. During their first lunch meeting, Georgiana made a plea for some professional assistance. Ms. Jackson was pleased to be considered a professional and was eager to help a motivated new teacher. She happily agreed to assume the role of unofficial mentor.

WEEKLY TEACHER-PARENT EMAIL

QUOTE FOR THE WEEK
"All children can learn! Nothing is so powerful as an idea whose time has come!" Victor Hugo

STUDY SUGGESTION FOR THE WEEK
Students who have their own designated place and time for quiet study and homework tend to develop the habit of work. Keep necessities, such as reference books and supplies appropriate to the student's age and grade level, handy. (Pencils, paper, eraser, calculator, markers and highlighters can be stored in a shoebox.)

HOMEWORK FOR THE WEEK
Monday: Read
Tuesday: Write
Wednesday: Calculate
Thursday: Construct
Friday: Interview

LOOKING AHEAD TO CLASS PROJECTS
1. In-depth study of our local environment. Preliminary pictures and observations presented on _____.
2. Small group research on specific topics to begin _____.

LOOKING AHEAD TO EVENTS
September 8: Parent/guardian Visitation and Orientation
October 2: Back to School for Parents

KEEP IN TOUCH
Use return email or phone (888-888-8888 after 3:30) for your comments or questions.

WHO'S WHO IN OUR CLASSROOM

Use your camera. Insert photos and names. Post on bulletin board.

Our teachers

Our students

WHO'S WHO IN OUR SCHOOL

Use your camera. Insert photos and names. Post on bulletin board.

Our principals

Our secretaries

Our nurses

Our custodians

Our cafeteria workers

Our security guards

Our guidance counselors

Our psychologists

Our librarians

WHO'S WHO IN OUR SCHOOL DISTRICT

Use your camera. Insert photos and names. Post on bulletin board.

Our superintendent

Our assistant superintendents

Our human resource director

Our special education directors

Our finance director

SAMPLE CLASSROOM RULES

1. Be in your seat on time.

2. Raise your hand for permission to speak or to leave your seat.

3. Always have your schoolwork supplies.

4. Bring your homework.

5. Talk respectfully.

6. Behave respectfully.

7. Do your best work.

8. Ask for help when you need it.

CLASSROOM EXPECTATIONS

Students need to know what you expect. Make your expectations clear and give them examples.

Situation	What to do
How should papers be headed?	Always put your heading _____. (location) Include _____. (information)
What should I do with papers that are returned to me?	Have your parent or guardian sign test papers and then put them in the appropriate subject area of your 3-ring binder.
What kind of supplies should I have?	You will need _____ spiral notebooks, a 3-ring binder, pencils, pens, highlighters, ruler, eraser, calculator and assignment pad.
What should I do if I am absent?	Bring a note explaining the reason for your absence. Check the homework chart to find out what you must make up. See me about when and where to get help with missing class assignments.
What should I do if I need to use the restroom? get a drink of water? go to the nurse?	Raise your hand to get a pass.
Can I bring water or soda to drink in class?	No food or drink is permitted in the classroom for health reasons.
What should I do with make-up work?	Put all make-up work in the bin on my desk marked "MAKE-UP WORK."
How will I know what the homework is?	The homework is always posted on the homework chart located _____.
When can I get extra help?	Extra help is available _____. (when and where)
Can I bring my cell phone to class?	Our classroom policy on cell phones is the same as the school policy which says that _____ _____.
Can I do my homework on my computer?	Yes! If you need help learning how to use the spell-check, please see me!
What do I do if I have to take medication?	All medication must be given to you by the _____.

5

Achieving Success with Collaborative Relationships

DON'T BUY THE DRESS YET!

Ariel looked around her fifth grade classroom with pride as she circulated the room assisting students. The 28 students were talking, perhaps a little more loudly than she would have liked, but obviously engaged in a science project testing the effectiveness of five popular cleaning agents on bacteria. She glanced over at her collaborating coteacher, Stan, and thought to herself, "Life is weird!"

That evening Ariel and her best friend, Julie, were discussing their teaching jobs over a take-out pizza when Ariel blurted out, "I can't believe it! I feel like I have been transported back to the days of arranged marriages."

"What on earth do you mean, Ariel? I give up! I haven't a clue what you're talking about this time!" Julie sighed as she grabbed another slice from the pizza box.

Ariel, in an exasperated tone replied, "Well, here I am a single independent woman. Realistically, at this point in my life, no one tells me who to associate with. My friends ask before making an effort to fix me up with their friends. I agree only if it interests me. A month ago, I joined an Internet dating site where, in quasi-scientific fashion using an application and interview form to discern my interests and values, matches are attempted."

"How many coteachers have had strong reservations about the person with whom they have been assigned to work?"

"Yeah, it's no secret how particular you are, but what are we talking about here, social life or professional life? So, is there a connection?" Julie questioned.

"Okay. Let me spell it out for you. You know me. I admit it. I am fussy. I pick and choose. I'd rather be alone than with someone who I can't connect with. So, what happens? I go to work, pick up my teaching schedule and find that the principal has arbitrarily decided I am going to be 'married' for the year. Further, he has decided with whom. No thought of personality traits, professional traits, likes or dislikes—just *do it*. For the next school year, Stan will be with me starting the day and ending the day. Imagine that, a stranger critiquing my every word and move. Frankly, I can't believe that this is what I have to do!"

"Aha, so that's what you mean! You and Stan! Your collaborating relationship may not be a marriage made in heaven. I get it! Don't buy the wedding dress yet."

If the truth were told, how many collaborators have had strong reservations about the person with whom they have been assigned to work? Someday some influential educator will make a revolutionary discovery that impacts on inclusion success: Success is directly dependent on the stability of the "marriage" of the collaborators! If and when all educators accept that fact and act accordingly, there will be serious improvement for *all* students involved in inclusion. In the meantime . . .

bottom line
■ ■ ■ ■ ■ ■ ■ ■ ■ ■

"To handle yourself, use your head; to handle others, use your heart."—Anonymous

As Ariel made clear, surprises are not always welcome! Certainly, a mandate to have a long-term, in-depth relationship that will seriously impact on your professional performance; affect your ability to inspire and connect with your students; and influence your mood, words and behavior can be a real source of irritation—if you let it! That I can affirm from personal experience working in collaborating relationships for ten years. I can also affirm that as long as we are who we are—employees and not the employer, teachers and not the administrator, and teachers who sincerely want to teach—we will accept our schedules, including surprise inclusion collaborators, and make the best of our situations.

This chapter is about how to maximize the success of the collaborative relationship you find yourself involved in. It is not about things you cannot control. It is not focused on the negative. It is focused on how to do your best to get the most positive results. You will find tips on how to maximize the cooperative effort for all the students in your class through the development of a positive relationship with your coteacher and paraprofessionals.

BRIGHT IDEA

Before meeting or planning with your coteacher, put first things first. Set aside some quiet time for personal reflection. Begin by establishing your own personal professional purpose. Write it down, with clear intent. Next, assess those aspects of your teaching job over which you have control and consider how you can best use those aspects to reach your own professional purpose. Picture your ideal teaching day; what are the "musts" in that picture? The "must nots"? Honestly consider your strengths and weaknesses as a teacher and as a soon-to-be collaborating teacher. After this picture takes on clarity, you are ready to welcome a colleague into your world.

Perhaps you don't yet know your collaborator personally, a situation experienced by many of us. You may know that you will be coteaching; you may have also been given the name of the coteacher. Nevertheless, it is entirely possible that the person with whom you will be sharing responsibilities is as new to you as you are to them. The good news about this is the number and variety of opportunities this situation affords you.

Of course, you want your school year to go smoothly. You recognize the importance of developing and maintaining a strong and positive collaborative relationship to enhance student learning and a peaceful teaching environment. This seems an ideal time to reflect on the research of Dr. Steven Covey, longtime revered relationship expert. Dr. Covey contends that first impressions are made within the first 30 seconds of an encounter, and although we don't want

bottom line

"It is our attitude at the beginning of a difficult undertaking which, more than anything else, will determine its outcome."— *William James*

"Considering that 80% of perception is formed by facial expression, tone of voice and body language, how important is that first encounter with your coteacher?"

to believe it, these impressions tend to last a lifetime. (Another world communication expert, Roger Ailes, reports that the first 7 seconds are critical in determining trust levels based on the verbal and nonverbal messages.) If they are both right about the speed at which impressions are made, that doesn't leave us much of a margin for error, does it?

Moreover, Dr. Covey believes we each keep an "emotional bank account" in which we store the positive or negative encounters we have with a person. This account is the one from which we draw our favorable or unfavorable feelings and which influences our behaviors. Finally, he observes that in our visual society, approximately 80% of perception is formed by facial expression, tone of voice and body language. Now I ask you, how important is that first encounter with your collaborator?

Getting collaboration off to a good start

Let's use Dr. Covey's helpful observations and consider some concrete tips for you to use in your coteaching:

- Smile, even if you are annoyed, aggravated or disappointed. Begin practicing optimism until it becomes a habit!

- Welcome collaborators not only with your smile, but also with your tone of voice, your body language and your actions. Share your space, emotional and physical.

- Show genuine interest in collaborators, personally and professionally. Be generous with your time, even if you feel pressured with other commitments. Listen to what they say and what they are conveying nonverbally. Try to make them feel at ease, knowing that they, too, are probably uncomfortable and unsure of how things will progress, how this "marriage" will work out.

bottom line

■ ■ ■ ■ ■ ■ ■ ■ ■ ■

"You can tell more about a person by what he says about others than you can by what others say about him."—
Leo Aikman

- Be prepared to laugh, especially at yourself. Resist any temptation to judge or criticize.

Tom Marshall, a "control" person with very pronounced opinions of his own worth, set a fine example of how *not* to establish a comfort zone for collaboration. Prior to the issuance of fall schedules, he was often heard in the cafeteria proclaiming, "No one is coming into *my* classroom and telling *my* students or *me* what to do. I am the king in my room!" Obviously, he was opposed to collaborating but just as obviously, his principal decided Tom would be a collaborator. Alexus Connally was the lucky person assigned to work with the self-proclaimed king. A spunky and optimistic teacher of five years, Alexus had heard about Tom's collaborative distaste, and although distressed to initiate any relationship with the monarch, she gave herself a little pep talk before heading down to what soon would be "their room." She knocked, walked in and cheerily introduced herself.

"One of the most critical elements of successful inclusive classrooms is a facilitating social/emotional climate in which students and teachers feel safe, valued and accepted. Such an environment promotes active participation and a sense of belonging." (Voltz, Brazil & Ford, 2001)

Tom scarcely acknowledged the door opening or the entry of Alexus. He remained seated, barely looked up from what he was doing and mumbled something that might have been "hello." He very effectively conveyed his feeling that she was an intruder in his kingdom. Alexus, already prepared for something less than a gala celebration, acutely felt his desire to have the upper hand and his attempt to relegate her to the role of supplicant. Rather than say or do something she would regret for the year, she briefly gave a synopsis of her professional experiences and indicated that she was pleased to have the opportunity to work with another professional. She then promptly made her departure, allowing herself to reflect further on how best to handle Tom and the future of the collaborating situation.

One way or another we survive the first day and first week of inclusion. I suspect there were moments when you wondered if you would, but if you were able to keep your critical comments to yourself, you may have learned a lot about your collaborator and about yourself. Hopefully, you will continue to employ the tips listed on page 94 as you work with your collaborator and students to establish a pleasant tone for

bottom line
■ ■ ■ ■ ■ ■ ■ ■ ■ ■

"The wishbone will never replace the backbone."— *Will Henry* classroom work. Please bear in mind your grandmother's advice: "Don't say anything if you can't say anything nice." Aim for "progress not perfection."

Keeping collaboration running smoothly

Here are some suggestions that worked for me. I feel confident they will help you.

- Continue to smile. Do everything possible to put fun into your day and into teaching, for you, your coteacher and, of course, your students. Success thrives in a happy, healthful environment.

- Continue to build trust with your collaborator by your regular and punctual attendance. If possible, arrive early to set up and prepare for students.

- Over-plan and over-prepare for collaboratively arranged lessons. Develop thoughtful and appropriate materials. Secure and set up the necessary AV equipment. Be certain that you are a master of the lesson topic.

- Treat your coteacher with courtesy and respect both in and out of the classroom. Do more than your share, voluntarily. Remember that a tiny seed of thoughtfulness can reap a harvest of good will.

- Determine a mutually convenient time for lesson planning. No matter how difficult it is, this is essential. (Some of us resort to email and iChat.)

- Keep the planning time focused and professional. Focus on the needs of all students. Thoughtfully include the students with special needs in all plans.

- Follow through on your commitments. Be prepared to assume full responsibility in the event of your coteacher's absence.

- Clearly delineate and agree on coteaching tasks. Be flexible enough to make any adjustments necessary. If preferred, rotate some routine chores or let particular skills and talents help determine how and what will be done.

bottom line
■ ■ ■ ■ ■ ■ ■ ■ ■ ■

"Success on any major scale requires you to accept responsibility . . . in the final analysis, the one quality that all successful people have . . . is the ability to take on responsibility."— *Michael Korda*

- Agree on the essentials: behavioral expectations (yours, your coteacher's, your students'), academic expectations, initial evaluation criteria (yours, your coteacher's, your students'), and specifically how and what responsibilities you will share.

- Lighten up. Admit your own mistakes. Laugh at yourself. Smile more. Enjoy teaching. Enjoy your coteacher. Enjoy *all* of your students. They will happily return the pleasure!

Inclusion teams come in many sizes, shapes and numbers. Some classrooms have one general and one special education coteacher. Some general education teachers are assigned one full-time paraprofessional with part-time assistance from a specialist. Most inclusion classes have a number of people, professional and paraprofessional, who work with students for a period of time during a day or during the week. Keeping track of who does what and when can be a daunting task. Moreover, successful inclusion requires more than keeping track. It demands a coordination of efforts, no matter what the time or space constraints.

BRIGHT IDEA

Consider using your lesson plans as an action log for the collaborating team. Check off who assumed responsibility for the different aspects of lessons. Make quick notes directly on your plans regarding strategies and techniques that were particularly successful or unsuccessful. Further, use your plans to stimulate discussion when you come together to evaluate your collaboration and student response and performance.

Sometimes it is the Committee on Special Education that determines how inclusion will take shape in your classroom. It may decide that a few of your special needs students need assistance from a paraprofessional. Certainly paraprofessionals can be invaluable to you and your students. Oftentimes they know the students, their families and the home environments better than do the teachers. Oftentimes they speak the native language and can be essential in forging better relationships with parents or guardians while uncovering real student or parental concerns.

Mrs. Garcia, a paraprofessional for five years, has a special needs child who the IEP committee decided to place in an inclusion classroom. Consequently, she intimately recognizes the unique inclusion classroom challenges. Fluent in Spanish and English, Mrs. Garcia is the contact person for Hispanic children who are not yet comfortable with English. Moreover, because she lives in the community with many of our students, she talks with parents and encourages them to become involved with their child's school. In the classroom, she circulates quietly, offering extra help or an encouraging word while assisting in the maintenance of an orderly and productive environment. Mrs. Garcia is a rare gem, well educated, thoughtful and optimistic. She seems to know instinctively who needs assistance and how much help to give. Nonetheless, this does not mean that regular collaboration is not essential. A team of professionals and paraprofessionals with differing goals and methods cannot automatically unite in their efforts. Planning is essential, even for one as skilled as Mrs. Garcia.

BRIGHT IDEA

Approximately 1 million paraprofessionals work in public schools tutoring, translating and helping with management issues under the direction of a qualified teacher. The well-informed and supervised paraprofessional can be an important tool in the education of students. (Keller, 2003)

In contrast, many of our paraprofessionals (a.k.a. paraeducators) come to the classroom showing enthusiasm but not knowing what to do or how to do it. Sometimes they even come with their own plan, certain that they know best! Without instruction and guidance, their presence in the classroom can be counterproductive, even disruptive, to the academic environment.

bottom line

"No one should teach who is not in love with teaching."—
Margaret E. Sangster

Nedra, a recent community college graduate, typifies a thorny collaborating situation. A highly attractive young woman in her early twenties, she arrived unexpectedly one morning, confident that she knew what to do. She walked in, introduced herself and then, without waiting for any direction, followed her own plans. All the sixth graders, male and female alike, were mesmerized by her cute distracting self, her trendy MTV clothing and shapely form. Not surprisingly, almost all vied for an opportunity for her "help." (I suspect several male teachers on the staff felt similarly!) Lessons stopped. Attention was focused on Nedra, who obviously was enjoying her role. If asked, the students would have had nothing but praise for Nedra.

BRIGHT IDEA

Wrightslaw (www.wrightslaw.com) suggests that teachers request "paraprofessionals" rather than "aides." There is no legal definition for aides; paraprofessionals must meet qualification standards. Paraprofessionals may work directly with students in a number of capacities as long as they are under the direct supervision of a teacher. Further, it is suggested that the CSE not assign a paraprofessional directly to a student, but rather to the classroom. In this way, the paraprofessional can encourage independent growth of the special needs student, when appropriate, while productively assisting others.

Let's face it. Yours is a challenging job. You are expected to ensure that all the students in your class thrive, behaviorally and academically. Given the wide range of abilities and disabilities in most inclusion classes, this is no simple feat. Further, you may be responsible for incorporating and supervising a number of paraprofessionals. You need the support and assistance of all who come into contact with your students. It would be great if you could pick and choose. You know, "I'll take Denise; she's bilingual, energetic and pleasant." But it rarely works that way. Support provided to you in the form of coteachers or paraprofessionals is determined by the person in charge of scheduling and tied to school district finances, inclusion commitment and availability of appropriate staff.

Teachers know that in this high stakes educational environment, where every classroom's progress or lack of it is not only monitored but shared with the public, all efforts must be directed toward one goal—the improvement of all student performance. Somehow we must learn to challenge and direct the Nedras to use their enthusiasm in a manner consistent with the team's goals. How to do it? The challenge is to bring the paraprofessionals onto the inclusion team, even if they are assigned for only a portion of the day.

bottom line
■ ■ ■ ■ ■ ■ ■ ■ ■ ■

"If you only care enough for a result, you will almost certainly achieve it."—*William James*

Working with paraprofessionals

Generally paraprofessionals report to you with expectations, concerns and probably considerable angst. They need your specific guidance and your suggestions about how to work as part of the inclusion team.

Empower your paraprofessional. Make certain that IEP and BIP documents are shared and discussed in planning how to work best with the special needs students. Devise a collaborative teamwork booklet that includes the following essential information:

"Empower your paraprofessional by discussing IEPs and BIPs when planning how to work best with your special needs students."

- What we do and how we do it in our classroom.
- Our rules.
- Survey of paraprofessional talents and skills.
- Opportunities for identifying concerns.
- Emergency procedures.
- Information clearly indicating means of regular communication.
- Guidelines for performance evaluation.
- Other pertinent information that will inform your paraprofessional about your efforts, goals and means of implementation.

I agree this sounds like an awful lot of work, but once done, your booklet can be reused and refined and save you time, energy and frustration. Most importantly, you will have helped the paraprofessional become part of your team.

BRIGHT IDEA

Paraprofessionals are assigned to a specific student, a specific program or a specific classroom and therefore will feel like a guest in your room. As with most guests they have concerns about expectations, manners, customs, likes and dislikes. Giving paraprofessionals specific direction and establishing a regular means of communicating can reduce anxiety, increase comfort level and promote productivity. (The Master Teacher, 1997)

Making your paraprofessional part of the team

I suggest that you consider your own personal comfort level, as well as the skill and comfort level of your paraprofessional, prior to determining which of the following are appropriate to your classroom situation. Further, I suggest that as trust and respect develop, roles may be redefined and expanded. The following list indicates ways your paraprofessional can support team efforts:

- Participating in collaborative team planning.
- Complementing classroom policies and customs.
- Redirecting off-task students.
- Quietly assisting a struggling student.
- Monitoring student behavior.
- Monitoring student academic performance.
- Reinforcing and helping students carry out daily living or self-help skills.
- Providing small group remedial or one-on-one instruction.
- Monitoring a behavior modification system.
- Making or modifying materials to meet special needs.
- Communicating with parents.
- Assisting students in making subject matter transitions.
- Assisting with daily routines and activities.
- Reinforcing previously instructed concepts.
- Documenting student progress.
- Modifying tasks and assignments.
- Helping with emergency procedures.
- Assisting with classroom management.
- Collecting data.
- Providing feedback to team members regarding performance or concerns.
- Becoming acquainted with students personally, understanding their behavioral and academic needs, and communicating critical information to team members.
- Identifying and communicating potential problems.
- Conversing in native language of student, as appropriate and necessary.
- Suggesting effective alternatives for instruction, interaction and management.
- Serving as role model and mentoring students.

bottom line
■ ■ ■ ■ ■ ■ ■ ■ ■ ■

"There is a real magic in enthusiasm. It spells the difference between mediocrity and accomplishment. It gives warmth and good feeling to all your personal relationships."— *Norman Vincent Peale*

Incorporating paraprofessionals into the inclusion team

Here are a few suggestions to help you make the most of the paraprofessionals on your inclusion team.

- Demonstrate your openness and pleasure that paraprofessionals will be part of the team by providing them with your respect and concern for their personal needs, concerns and abilities. Check that physical space for belongings and a work area are available.

- Initiate a means of regular communication even if they are unavailable to meet personally with the team. Sticky notes, emails and iChat are options that may work well.

- Encourage paraprofessionals to share observations and helpful criticisms important to the success of students and the collaborative effort.

- Agree on and role model the most professional and appropriate way for students and team members to refer to paraprofessionals. Be certain to use correct titles.

- Recognize their gifts and contributions when speaking to colleagues and students. Show your appreciation to students, colleagues and administrators as well as the paraprofessionals themselves.

- Treat them in a professional manner. Share goals, operating procedures and expectations. Support them with resources that will enable professional growth.

LEGAL ALERT

Supervising paraprofessionals, as well as working as part of a collaborative teaching team, may be a new experience for you. Did you know that those school districts receiving funds from the Improving Teacher Quality State Grants (affiliated with No Child Left Behind Act) are *mandated* to ask teaching staff to determine how to spend the professional development money? Here's an opportunity for you to suggest professional development in collaborative teaching issues.

Evaluating collaboration and its impact on students

It would not be responsible to conclude this chapter on collaborating without devoting a portion to evaluation of your team. I am a firm believer in evaluation—evaluation of most everything. Too often we assume we are doing well, making progress, without any objective information to substantiate our assumption. If we don't assess our teaching, our students' academic and behavioral progress and our collaborating efforts, we may never realize we are off track. Continual critical evaluation, informal or formal, written or oral, will provide information to help us move forward positively. Your willingness to be self-critical and demonstrate sincere interest in professional improvement helps develop trust with team members. Importantly, keep your humor and positive attitude during any evaluation process.

BRIGHT IDEA

Be realistic in expectations of your paraprofessional. Bear in mind that paraprofessionals do not yet have your professional education and expertise. Importantly, new legislation mandates that paraprofessionals achieve new levels of training and competence. You can help them in this regard by demonstrating professional behavior and by sharing your professional resources. Further, be aware that their pay scale is too often embarrassingly low.

Here are a few ideas to help you evaluate your collaboration efforts:

- Develop a "pre-nuptial agreement" in which you objectively state and agree on essential personal and professional behaviors and strategies. Agree to deal immediately, and as dispassionately as possible, with any personal or professional concerns that could impede student growth or your collaborative relationship.

- Develop objective criteria for evaluating your inclusion progress, collaboration successes and failures, and student successes. Establish collaborative evaluation as a daily

bottom line
■ ■ ■ ■ ■ ■ ■ ■ ■ ■

"Opportunity is missed by most people because it is dressed in overalls and looks like work."— *Thomas A. Edison* expectation for quick assessment of student behavioral and academic response to your instruction and certainly your collaborative efforts.

- Take time for a more in-depth weekly evaluation to modify strategies, presentation styles and responsibilities. Ask how you could better assist and teach. Resist the temptation to be negative or demeaning. Criticism can be helpful only when it is positive and constructive.

- If you and your coteacher are risk takers, consider soliciting comments from your students. If students feel that they are an integral part of the teaching and learning and that their ideas are valued, you will find that shared progress will take on a new meaning and seriousness for all. Caution! Be prepared for the unusual candor of students. At times, students notice behaviors that adults might not. It might be helpful for you to ask students to help you develop a simple rubric for evaluating a teacher. This way you can encourage objectivity and involvement, which will open the doors to further group efforts.

bottom line
■ ■ ■ ■ ■ ■ ■ ■ ■ ■

"No mistakes, no experience; no experience, no wisdom."—
Stanley Goldstein

Power of One

The Challenge

Alexus Connally was early for the third mandated in-service training session on inclusion. She selected a seat at a table and began to organize herself for the session. One of her colleagues, seated at a nearby table, bent over and yelled, "Hey, Alexus, how's life with royalty? Does Tom wear his crown to class as a reminder of his regal background?"

Alexus had had a rough day with her coteacher and was sorely tempted to respond. Tom had seemed especially hell-bent on provoking her in what appeared to be an effort to force the smile off her face. Having survived the day, part of her felt the need to vent and let her exasperation show. She mentally savored the pleasure of making a few pithy and critical remarks. "What to do?" she asked herself.

The Response

You can be pretty certain that Alexus would have had a captive audience for any and all critical comments about Tom. She could develop a support group of her peers by belittling Tom's attitudes and demeaning his behaviors. Fortunately, she did not. Her short-term pleasure (and revenge) would yield long-term problems because her comments would eventually get back to Tom. Any positive "emotional bankroll" that she was working hard to develop, any progress toward building a trusting professional relationship, would be destroyed. Her peers would not soon forget that even the optimistic and professional Alexus could and would gossip with the best of them!

COLLABORATING TEAM WEEKLY EVALUATION

We suggest that collaborating team members evaluate progress weekly to continually improve efforts. Use this form as a guide to help you objectively discuss your work.

	Strongly agree	Agree	Unsure	Disagree	Strongly disagree
1. The inclusion lessons were well planned.	☐	☐	☐	☐	☐
2. Instruction in the class was agreed on collaboratively.	☐	☐	☐	☐	☐
3. The coteaching styles worked well together. Why? Why not? When?	☐	☐	☐	☐	☐
4. Special education and regular education students benefited from the instruction. If not, why not? What could have been done differently?	☐	☐	☐	☐	☐
5. The special education teacher modified instruction to meet student needs.	☐	☐	☐	☐	☐
6. The special education teacher modified materials to meet student needs.	☐	☐	☐	☐	☐
7. Modifications and planning were appropriate to all students.	☐	☐	☐	☐	☐
8. Communication with students was fair, appropriate and effective.	☐	☐	☐	☐	☐
9. Rules were enforced and discipline was handled consistently. We all worked together on classroom management.	☐	☐	☐	☐	☐
10. The general and special educators communicated differences and concerns in a constructive manner.	☐	☐	☐	☐	☐
11. Team members were flexible in adjusting assignments, planning curricula and developing instructional strategies.	☐	☐	☐	☐	☐
12. The team projects a positive feeling about inclusion.	☐	☐	☐	☐	☐

■ What are the strong points of our collaborative effort?

■ What are the weak points of our collaborative effort?

■ How can our team better prepare and accomplish curricular objectives?

■ What can we do more effectively?

PREFERRED TEACHING STYLE INVENTORY

Consider the manner in which you teach. Divide the circle below into tenths. Label each segment to indicate the time during an average class period you spend on the following:

1. Lecture
2. Note-taking
3. Group work
4. Demonstrations
5. Reading (silent, oral)
6. Lab work or independent work
7. Audio-video presentation
8. Computer work
9. Worksheets
10. Group discussions

Compare your circle with that of your coteacher. Make adjustments for optimal collaboration, considering the students with special needs.

COLLABORATING TEAM
SCHOOL READINESS SURVEY

Be aware of the potential for inclusion support in your school. The National Information Center for Children and Youth with Disabilities (NICHCY) recommends components for successful inclusion. Rank the readiness of your school. (Keep your included students in mind as your frame of reference.)

	Effective— already in place	Fair— on way to goal	Poor— still a dream
1. A method for evaluating student progress—academic, social and behavioral.	☐	☐	☐
2. A method for evaluating the inclusion program and its effectiveness.	☐	☐	☐
3. A program to develop and promote school-wide awareness of disability needs and to encourage an atmosphere of acceptance.	☐	☐	☐
4. A general education student body that is informed, aware and accepting of inclusion.	☐	☐	☐
5. High expectations for all students.	☐	☐	☐
6. Ongoing staff training in inclusion.	☐	☐	☐
7. Classroom support in terms of resources, planning time, space, supplementary aids and devices, and additional staff as needed.	☐	☐	☐
8. Access to assistive technology, including up-to-date computers.	☐	☐	☐
9. Rules enforced consistently, with everyone working together on classroom management.	☐	☐	☐
10. Adaptations to the curriculum to promote participation of the included students.	☐	☐	☐
11. A fair, consistent discipline policy for all students.	☐	☐	☐
12. A planning team to maintain coordination of efforts, to troubleshoot, to promote effective school-home communication and to solve problems creatively.	☐	☐	☐

■ Who can support our efforts to make positive changes?

COLLABORATING TEAM CLASSROOM GUIDE

We often assume that students, coteachers and paraprofessionals know the classroom rules, regulations and expectations. Not so. Collaborating team members should agree on how students should handle the following situations. Next, review them, as appropriate, with the students. (Use this guide with substitute teachers so classroom continuity will be assured.)

Here's a guide and contract of expectations for this class. As we review procedures, complete the phrase at the left by finishing the sentence in the box at the right. Please sign and have your parent or guardian sign to signify that the procedures are understood.

Scenario	Expectation
1. When I enter class, I should . . .	
2. After I have completed the above (#1), while I wait for the teacher to begin the class, I should/may . . .	
3. If I am late to class, I should . . .	
4. If homework is due, I should . . . (Include where, when and how it should be submitted.)	
5. If I have to use the restroom, I should . . .	
6. If I have neglected to complete a class assignment or homework, I should . . .	
7. If an emergency requires me to leave the classroom, I should . . .	
8. My work will be graded on the following . . .	
9. I will know my homework assignment because . . .	
10. If I want to hand in a makeup assignment or extra credit work, I should . . .	
11. If I am absent for a test, I should . . .	
12. If I need extra help, I should . . .	

Date: _____ Student signature: _____

Parent/guardian signature: _____

Please feel free to write any questions or comments!

CRITERIA FOR COLLABORATIVE HARMONY

Small everyday courtesies or irritations can make or break a coteaching team. Below are some items that are important to consider. Two columns have been provided, one for each coteacher. Take time to reflect before responding. Answer honestly, and then share and discuss with your coteacher.

	Coteacher 1	Coteacher 2
1. When do you arrive to class? a. Early. b. At the beginning of class or school. c. Usually a little late. d. Other. Explain.		
2. How would you describe your preparedness for the day's lessons? a. Knowledgeable and ready to begin. b. Fuzzy about the subjects but ready to wing it. c. Haven't a clue what the lessons are about. d. Other. Explain.		
3. To what extent do you take charge of the situation? a. I am always in charge. b. I am flexible and take charge when necessary or appropriate. c. I do not take charge. d. Other. Explain.		
4. To what extent do you smile and demonstrate courtesy to your coteacher? a. I make a point of greeting my coteacher with a smile and speaking politely. b. I am usually too rushed but I try to. c. I mean to, but I forget. d. Other. Explain.		
5. How would you describe the manner in which you interact with your coteacher in front of students? a. Professionally and with humor and courtesy. b. The period often goes by without any interaction. c. I don't think about it. d. Other. Explain.		
6. How would you describe your attendance? a. Infrequently absent. b. Absent once or more a month. c. Absent frequently. d. Other. Explain.		

COLLABORATING TEAM SELF-EVALUATION

The following items are meant as a guide for effective collaboration. Please take a few minutes for self-evaluation. If you feel comfortable, you may share your responses with your collaborators. If not, be certain to speak up about any concerns you have regarding the collaborating efforts, especially any feeling of lack of trust.

Yes No

☐ ☐ 1. I arrive to class prior to the bell.

☐ ☐ 2. I greet my coworker and students with a smile.

☐ ☐ 3. I follow and encourage students to follow the class rules.

☐ ☐ 4. I know what is expected of me each period.

☐ ☐ 5. I am able to follow my coworker's nonverbal cues.

☐ ☐ 6. I feel free to communicate my concerns, ideas and comments.

☐ ☐ 7. I can identity and assist those students in need of specific academic or behavioral help.

☐ ☐ 8. I guide students rather than provide answers or do the work for them.

☐ ☐ 9. I am aware of classroom operating procedures and can answer student questions about them.

☐ ☐ 10. I support my coworkers disciplinary efforts and guidelines.

☐ ☐ 11. I maintain confidentiality in regard to students' personal and academic history.

☐ ☐ 12. I help daily to enhance the academic instruction of the class.

☐ ☐ 13. I feel comfortable asking for explanation or assistance from my coworker.

☐ ☐ 14. Students seem to be accepting and respectful of me.

☐ ☐ 15. I feel comfortable working with my coworker.

☐ ☐ 16. I feel comfortable helping all students.

☐ ☐ 17. I would like to discuss this self-evaluation with my coworker.

☐ ☐ 18. I would like to take part in and provide input into my professional evaluation.

☐ ☐ 19. I have read student IEPs and abide by them.

☐ ☐ 20. I know if a student has a BIP and what is stipulated in it.

■ One question that I want answered is . . .

■ If I could change one thing, it is . . .

■ I could be a more effective member of this collaborating team if . . .

PARAPROFESSIONAL SKILL-COMFORT CHECKLIST

Working with others collaboratively can be more effective and comfortable when team members recognize their skills and talents while accepting those areas that are not within their comfort zone. Please respond to the following, indicating your level of comfort. Your additional comments are appreciated.

	Very comfortable	Fairly comfortable	Unsure	Uncomfortable	Very uncomfortable
1. Providing one-on-one instruction.	☐	☐	☐	☐	☐
2. Reading passages or instructions.	☐	☐	☐	☐	☐
3. Rewording or simplifying passages and instructions for ease of comprehension.	☐	☐	☐	☐	☐
4. Providing small group instruction (using teacher instruction and guidance).	☐	☐	☐	☐	☐
5. Refocusing and redirecting off-task students.	☐	☐	☐	☐	☐
6. Assisting students with specific disabilities.	☐	☐	☐	☐	☐
7. Understanding or speaking a second language.	☐	☐	☐	☐	☐
8. Reinforcing previously taught concepts.	☐	☐	☐	☐	☐
9. Using a computer for word processing.	☐	☐	☐	☐	☐
10. Using a computer for research (Internet skills).	☐	☐	☐	☐	☐
11. Using a scientific calculator.	☐	☐	☐	☐	☐
12. Helping with advanced math concepts.	☐	☐	☐	☐	☐
13. Helping with disciplinary issues and affirming class rules.	☐	☐	☐	☐	☐
14. Relating to and working with ED students.	☐	☐	☐	☐	☐
15. Maintaining a calm attitude even if provoked.	☐	☐	☐	☐	☐
16. Accepting constructive criticism.	☐	☐	☐	☐	☐
17. Giving constructive criticism.	☐	☐	☐	☐	☐
18. Assisting with group projects.	☐	☐	☐	☐	☐
19. Reading nonverbal cues.	☐	☐	☐	☐	☐
20. Sharing responsibility for instruction.	☐	☐	☐	☐	☐
21. Helping provide specified testing modifications.	☐	☐	☐	☐	☐
22. Encouraging students toward independence.	☐	☐	☐	☐	☐
23. Following collaborator's guidelines and lessons.	☐	☐	☐	☐	☐
24. Making materials (modifying, copying, etc.).	☐	☐	☐	☐	☐
25. Assisting with emergency evacuation plans.	☐	☐	☐	☐	☐

■ My special skills and talents:

■ Ways I can be most effective:

COLLABORATING TEAM
COMMUNICATION NOTICE

Daily communication enhances relationships and instruction. You are in a position to strengthen the team's effectiveness. When you have valuable information, kindly use the form below for conveying it. Place the comments [in our mailbox, on the desk or other specified location]. If you feel a sense of urgency about something, please be certain to share it immediately!

1. Today I heard, saw or felt the following that I think it is important for you to know:

_____

_____

_____

_____

_____

2. I have a concern about . . . _____

_____

_____

_____

_____

3. I am pleased that . . . _____

_____

_____

_____

_____

6

Developing an Optimal Learning Environment

JR. DH

Darwin, a.k.a. Jr. Dee Hop, seemed always to be in motion, truly a commanding fourth grader on the move. If the class was lining up to go to lunch, you could be certain that Jr. DH, as the kids called him, would be organizing and entertaining as they made their way to the cafeteria. Any outside observer would immediately notice that the class was under the leadership, not of the teacher, but of this slight ball of energy found at the front of the class. Rather than in straight lines, 27 young bodies seemed to be jiving down the hall in waves behind Jr. DH. No, there was not a voice to be heard, but hand signs and dancing feet definitely united the happy group.

Mike Davis, one of the coteachers of this inclusion class, found himself redefining his own teaching role since Jr. DH had naturally taken over the management of the class. Never before had Mike seen one youngster so able to captivate, motivate and bond a group of peers. Admittedly, he found Jr. to be one of the funniest kids he had ever encountered. Additionally, he was astounded with how the students looked forward to each day's lessons, enlivened by the curiosity and responses of Jr. DH. Teaching had become what he always dreamed it might be, a real adventure and a joy, thanks to the classroom atmosphere created by Jr. DH. Further, he and his coteacher, Mrs. Wright, agreed that this was the easiest group of youngsters to teach, even though there were eight special needs students, one of which was Jr. DH.

"How many teachers have enough strength to allow a student's natural leadership to help balance discipline and learning?"

Nonetheless, Mike Davis and Mrs. Wright had to deal with a number of dilemmas, including the daily trip through the school halls to lunch. They were well aware that the administration felt there should be a traditional decorum marking the progression to the cafeteria. They also realized that, more than likely, their personal classroom management techniques were being scrutinized and probably criticized as well. So be it, they decided. Let the positive academic and behavioral progress of the students serve as their response to criticism.

How many of us have enough personal strength and conviction to allow the natural leadership talent of a student to help us balance discipline and learning in the classroom? Indeed, a student such as Jr. DH is a rare gem, the likes of which you may encounter only once over a long teaching career, and is a poignant reminder that a student with serious special needs can also possess extraordinary gifts. Such a student brings not only a thrill to teaching but confusion to the definition of the teaching role. Should you allow a Jr. the latitude to embrace the class and use your framework to manage the class? Or, should you claim firm control and squelch his ebullient attitude? At what point can such a student, indeed any student, be the fulcrum that provides the balance in a diverse group of learners?

bottom line
■ ■ ■ ■ ■ ■ ■ ■ ■ ■

Consider personal growth toward improved self-control as part of your classroom management program.

This chapter is devoted to the one topic most teachers feel is the bane of their professional career—classroom management. Working with your collaborators to develop a repertoire of techniques and strategies for dealing with the myriad personalities and attitudes you face can be an eye-opening experience. The process begins with you, with coming to terms with your personality, your self-confidence, your control issues, your tolerance, your humor and your tenacity. Recognition of all these factors is essential before beginning to determine collaboratively what is acceptable and unacceptable as together your team forges a classroom management plan.

I think most teachers would agree that disciplinary problems get in the way of effective teaching and productive learning. Unfortunately, there is no "one size fits all" strategy for success in managing a classroom of diverse students. There are, however, strategies and techniques that have proven valuable in providing the structure from which to build a management plan appropriate to the styles, personalities and needs of both teachers and students.

Over the years of my professional career, I have been exposed to the advice and techniques of many, many teachers. Thus far, I have concluded that there is no one best management method. What I have come to understand is that a successful discipline program is structured to maximize the time teachers and students share. The message is twofold: (1) Time spent together must be well spent toward clearly defined rigorous academic and behavioral goals, and (2) a shared student-staff commitment to a harmonious, helpful relationship promotes academic and behavioral growth for all. When students and teachers work as a team, together they have a stake in making the team succeed.

Developing a framework for inclusion classroom management

Trial and error can promote powerful learning. During the course of my career, I have had many classroom disciplinary challenges (otherwise known as "problems"). As with most problems we encounter, we have a choice: Stay anchored in the problems or use them as opportunities for growth. For me, I am always anxious to move away from pain! Consequently, I have continually searched for the means to augment my repertoire. Thanks to sharing with and learning from other teachers, conducting research and experimenting day-to-day, I have been able to develop a large repertoire of responses from which to choose. This

bottom line
■ ■ ■ ■ ■ ■ ■ ■ ■ ■

The pessimist looks at opportunities and sees difficulties; the optimist looks at difficulties and sees opportunities.— *Anonymous* has allowed me to tailor my response more appropriately to the situation and the student.

Averting discipline problems

Following are criteria for an effective behavioral management framework that will help avert discipline problems:

1. Always recognize personal worth. Respect engenders respect. The time you spend getting to know each student is invaluable. Time spent allowing students to get to know you and each other at the beginning of the term allows you all to bond, while promoting trust in a safe and accepting environment.

BRIGHT IDEA

When bad habits are deeply ingrained, they take time to change (indeed, some you may never change). Give students opportunities to practice, to observe positive peer role models and to enjoy praise for appropriateness. Accept that all students may not become model students! If you have neither the training nor the time to deal with serious emotional or aggressive behavior, seek out the school psychologist, a guidance counselor, a talented colleague or an administrator for assistance. Do not be afraid to ask for help.

Mrs. Sharon did not subscribe to this notion. She felt that her role as teacher, the authority, was sufficient to ensure that students would give her respect and do as they were told. Somehow it just doesn't work that way. Not only did Mrs. Sharon disrespect her students with her yelling, grouchy demeanor and unkind comments ("What a stupid thing to say!" she responded to one fifth grader who remarked that the assignment was confusing), she also disrespected her own peers! When disciplinary problems mounted, she was unable to accept her responsibility for their cause. Instead she always pointed fingers to some student who, she insisted, must be emotionally disturbed!

bottom line

Teachers who disrespect students, earn student disrespect.

2. Appreciate diversity of talents, cultural backgrounds, learning styles and interests. Encourage students to acknowledge that although we may look different and learn differently, we all can benefit from each other by sharing our individual gifts. A team attitude of acceptance is paramount.

3. Self-control is mandatory. Teachers are the role models; out-of-control teachers can expect an out-of-control classroom. Our very human nature guarantees that at some time, some student, in some way will irritate the heck out of us. Again here is that opportunity to choose— do we retaliate or do we pause and reflect? Needless to say, the professional choice is to reflect and consider options before saying or doing anything. You will find that some of your special needs students may bring unusual and exasperating behaviors into your classroom. Try to use them as personal growth opportunities!

4. Establish and follow routines so students know what to expect. Plan how you will assist students who have difficulty making transitions from one activity to the next.

5. Collaboratively develop and post the classroom rules, stated simply and affirmatively, in a conspicuous place. Preferably, involve the class in determining the essential rules for a positive working classroom environment. When an infraction occurs refer quietly and personally to the number of the rule and suggest a more appropriate behavior. Do not expect all students to immediately conform. Role modeling is most effective. Endeavor to enforce the rules consistently, using appropriate consequences. Be certain that even the adult members of the inclusion team adhere to rules and high performance standards.

Mike was part of a collaborating team, one of the paraprofessionals assigned for two class periods before heading off to another classroom. He was an easygoing, affable young man who was eager to help, but he had two irritating habits: (1) He reported to class just a little late, and (2) he always entered drinking his coffee from the cafeteria. It didn't take long for the students to point out that he was breaking the rules. Indeed, he was. Fortunately he had the good humor to make a learning experience out of it, for himself and the class. If we had not established a strong rapport early on, he may not have been so accepting and the class so open in commenting!

"Endeavor to enforce the rules consistently, using appropriate consequences."

bottom line
■ ■ ■ ■ ■ ■ ■ ■ ■ ■

The only control you have in the classroom is the control you have over yourself.

6. Do try to remember that rules are in place to promote harmony and student achievement. This assumes that there is a rigorous academic program in place that engages and enthuses all students. It assumes that students know they will be provided with necessary assistance and are expected to perform to the best of their ability, stay on task and encourage others to do the same. Unplanned, idle time encourages misbehavior.

BRIGHT IDEA

Take care to respect the unique needs of all students. Be certain not to use labels or classifications when talking to a student or about a student. Never single out a student, special needs or not, for criticism in front of peers. Try to objectify misbehavior, demonstrating how it interferes with the lesson and personal as well as class progress. Optimally, this means developing a habit of conferencing with any student who is infringing on important classroom rules. The positive result from such demonstrated respect on your part will yield much improved behavior on the student's part.

Charles Devereaux thought he could get by with a few sketchy lesson plans; after all, how hard can it be to teach fifth grade? Each day he chatted with students about any topic they brought up and then incidentally eased into some sort of lesson that touched on the subject. Students, particularly those with special needs, invariably became restless and talkative, then actively involved in misbehavior. When asked why, they responded: "We aren't learning anything anyway. What does it matter?" Mr. Devereaux responded: "Those special education kids don't belong in here. They're nothing but trouble."

7. Make every effort to be nonjudgmental. Some students are dealing with overwhelming home problems such as alcoholism, drug abuse and abandonment and are doing a better job of coping than we might! Try to separate distress over the behavior from distress over the student. Reinforce acceptable and appropriate behavior while quietly discouraging misbehavior.

8. De-escalate tension and negativism with humor, no matter how corny. Laughter reduces stress for you and for the students. Make it clear that you are not laughing

bottom line
■ ■ ■ ■ ■ ■ ■ ■ ■ ■

You grow up the day you have your first real laugh at yourself.—
Ethel Barrymore

at someone but at a situation or at yourself. Make each day a new day and a brand new opportunity. Smile. Hold no grudges.

BRIGHT IDEA

Set aside daily stress-breaking time, working out at the gym, cycling, meditating or doing yoga—whatever allows you a physical outlet and quiet reflective time. These refreshing times will be restorative and improve your effectiveness. Allot a reasonable amount of after-school time for schoolwork, and stick to it! Make it a habit to focus and complete the priority items. You will find that you work smarter and accomplish more.

9. Avoid the bait. If you have a student skilled in adversarial techniques who takes pleasure in trying to engage you in argument, opt out. Endless debate is a power struggle that will consume needed instructional time and ultimately serves no positive purpose. Establish, explain and abide by the established classroom structure. Extend an invitation to the student to join you in continuing the discussion after school.

10. Start and end the day with a smile. Make time to greet students by name at the door. Make time at the conclusion of your time together to send them off with a cheerful personal word. Teachers who are liked and respected have far fewer management issues and far greater opportunities for promoting student academic success.

11. Be aware of environmental distractions that divert student attention. Sometimes even oral reading or recitations can stand in the way of a special needs student's ability to focus on assigned work. Take into account student needs, abilities, gender and social skills when designing seating plans or group activities.

12. Consider the performance level of each student, and provide needed curricular modifications. Assignments that are inappropriate to a student's ability level can cause frustration and ultimately to misbehavior.

bottom line
■■■■■■■■■■

You give little when you give of your possessions. It is when you give of yourself that you truly give.—
Kahlil Gibran

Dealing with potentially serious discipline problems

I hate to admit it, but there are times when students will push you to the very limit. Those are the times you most need your personal arsenal of responses to inappropriate, even dangerous, behavior. It only takes one-out-of-control, troubled student to turn your class into a zoo. For that reason I suggest you think carefully about the following suggestions for your own safety and that of those sharing your classroom.

1. Make certain all team members are familiar with the IEPs of the special needs students to ascertain that the plans are being followed. Such things as individual or group weekly counseling may be written into the plan and offer the student needed relief and help. Remember that the IEP is a legal document. You do not have a choice about following it.

2. Use your classroom timeout area as a cooling off area for any student in need of time to calm down. Make every effort to avoid stigmatizing the special needs student by calling attention to the student or the misbehavior. Generally, the more normal the treatment, the more normal the behavior. Bear in mind that to use a school designated timeout room, the

LEGAL ALERT

IDEA sets forth standards for disciplining special needs students. There is nothing in the law that interferes with a school disciplining a special needs student. Indeed, not to address behavior dangerous to self or others could be cause to claim that the present placement is not an "appropriate educational environment." The recent reauthorization of IDEA reaffirms that schools have a responsibility to provide a safe, violence-free learning environment for all. Consequently, all students must be taught the code of discipline and recognize the consequences for inappropriate behavior.

For special needs students, this means that strategies, supports and interventions must be written into the IEP to address any behavior that impedes learning. If a pattern of problematic behavior develops, the IEP team should determine if modifications to the IEP are necessary. Incidents involving weapons, drug sales or drug use require immediate administrative attention. The administration is responsible for handling such serious issues. Contact them immediately regarding seriously inappropriate behaviors.

IEP must specify that the timeout room is an alternative for the specified student.

3. Check all the IEPs carefully. If there is a Behavior Intervention Plan (BIP), be certain that you abide by the recommendations. I have found that BIPS can offer prosocial tips helpful in dealing with problems related to all students, not just special needs students. Being proactive by using positive interventions reduces the need to be reactive due to negative behaviors.

"BIPS can offer prosocial tips for dealing with problems related to all students, not just special needs students."

4. Never touch a student. Students know their "rights," especially the more troubled ones who perhaps have had the unfortunate experience of being cycled through several foster homes or who have endured abusive behavior from parents or guardians.

   This I can attest to: Even a well-meaning pat on the arm to reinforce a positive behavior can cause unexpected results. An example is Charles, a special needs child with serious emotional difficulties. There was talk from the kids that he was the recipient of abuse from a stepfather with a violent temper, but just talk. I quickly learned that Charles had a difficult time with any type of attention, so I always took care not to draw attention to him. We had developed a rather comfortable manner of coexisting that, unfortunately, I unwittingly and unsuspectingly disturbed. One day after Charles had done particularly well on his math lesson, I stopped at his desk and quietly praised his work while touching him on the arm. Bad move on my part. He went berserk, yelling that I was abusing him and that I would hear from his father. Indeed he was true to his word. It took the skill of a guidance counselor, an administrator and myself to convince the livid father who arrived the next day to "take me on" that Charles had in no way been abused.

5. Never corner a student, either physically or emotionally. You will lose face and waste time and energy. Further, the student may win the emotional struggle in the eyes of his peers, leaving you with an additional problem to overcome. I have found that humor or calm deflection of focus is far more effective.

bottom line
■ ■ ■ ■ ■ ■ ■ ■ ■ ■

Our ultimate measure as people is not where we stand in moments of comfort and convenience, but where we stand during challenge and controversy.— *Martin Luther King, Jr.*

6. Be certain that you never tutor or talk with a student in a classroom without another colleague or student present. Further, never transport a student in your car. One accusatory comment about your behavior can result in a lawsuit or the loss of your professional status.

7. Accusing, threatening, screaming or using sarcasm with students is counterproductive. Such teacher behaviors may escalate problems and certainly will undo any positive influence you have as a role model.

8. Never make threats or give empty warnings. Use your repertoire of selected and appropriate consequences that are enforceable.

As much as you want to be able to use the same consequence for rule infraction for all student misbehavior, I suspect it will not be possible in all cases. Certainly, inclusion classes have a wide range of student abilities and disabilities. Use intuition and experience as a guide. The stronger the bond with students, the better teachers are able to determine an appropriate and meaningful response for a particular student to a particular situation.

BRIGHT IDEA

If you have volatile students who have not yet learned to control their temper, it is important to give them physical and emotional space. If you find that you must confront these students, do it without "getting in their face." Position yourself at an angle rather than head on and quietly offer alternatives, for example, "please sit down" or "see me after school."

bottom line
■ ■ ■ ■ ■ ■ ■ ■ ■ ■

Make every day a new day. Try not to hold grudges against students.

9. Take advantage of parental wisdom and support. Parents and guardians want success, academic and behavioral, for their children. If you are regularly communicating your goals and encouraging parental involvement, together you can reinforce each other's efforts. Together you can discuss techniques and strategies that have or have not worked, thereby saving time and energy while amplifying positive results. It is tempting to notify parents or guardians only about negative behaviors and performance, but alerting them to encouraging growth demonstrates genuine concern.

10. Focus on violence prevention. Be proactive rather than reactive. Start the year with your emergency discipline plan intact and familiar to all collaborators. Know which teachers, administrators or security people you can count on for immediate help. Establish procedures for (1) getting responsible assistance to your room immediately, (2) removing an out-of-control student and (3) vacating your room immediately.

Handling specific discipline problems

The following table provides pointers for handling the annoying behaviors that can disrupt classroom learning. Even elementary students have had plenty of time and experience in developing effective ways of communicating. I'm sure you have noticed how skilled some are at pushing your buttons to get a response. Teachers have an added challenge to try to determine whether the motivation behind the student's behavior is such that professional assistance is required to deal with the given situation. Assuredly, there are many variations on each of the following themes. You will find that patience, a dispassionate response and your concern for the student and your class are essential.

bottom line
■ ■ ■ ■ ■ ■ ■ ■ ■ ■

One thing I know, the only ones among you who will be really happy are those who will have sought and found how to serve.—
Albert Schweitzer

Problem	Possible cause	Possible response
The Curser: Student uses profanity with peers and teachers. Sets a poor behavioral example, upsets the teacher, may entertain the class. Can be contagious. If allowed to continue, may undermine management plan and demean the teacher's role.	May be intentional or unintentional. Student may or may not perceive it as disrespectful. Could be a power tool to claim attention, control or to change the focus of attention.	Control anger. Attempt to determine motive. Do not demean student. State privately that swearing is unacceptable. Give a warning and, if unheeded, a consequence. Determine consequence based on motive. Help student develop alternative for swear words, even a humorous word as replacement. Change will be slow.
The Disrespecter: Student continually puts down teacher and peers, verbally or nonverbally. Student talks back and is unkind and inconsiderate to all. Behavior changes classroom environment. Peers and teacher may feel threatened, angry, rejected or abused. Teacher who allows behavior to continue is diminished in eyes of other students.	Pervasive anger. Desire for revenge. May be disrespected in own life and has developed the habit in dealing with others. May indicate lack of understanding or empathy for others or an effort to assume power. May feel inadequate or have little self-esteem.	Do not corner student, either emotionally or physically. Retain a calm, professional demeanor. Confront student quietly and personally, stating that the behavior is unacceptable. Offer alternatives. Do *not* permit the behavior to continue. Counsel student after school or class. Do not retaliate. Keep focus on student progress and student responsibility for changing behavior. Try to develop personal relationship to build trust, or seek a staff member who might be able to forge positive relationship. Develop plan to give student opportunities for success, even if small. Seek assistance from guidance counselor, dean of students or psychologist, if necessary.

Problem	Possible cause	Possible response
The Impulsive Student: Student acts or speaks first, thinks later. Seems unable to restrain self. Has difficulty staying on task and following directions. Disruptions to lessons interfere with class progress. Distracting behaviors cause peer distraction that may result in misbehavior. Aggravating to teacher. Becomes habitual. Can be contagious.	Could be multihandicapped, ADD or ADHD. Could have language deficiencies or difficulty understanding expectations. Could be seeking attention.	Attempt to show student frequency of misbehavior and ramifications to self and class. Encourage self-monitoring program. Try to determine what precedes misbehavior and anticipate problem by alerting student with a cue. Try to refocus student or move closer to provide assistance or attention. Perhaps ignore some of the negative to begin focusing on the positive. Seat student near positive, compliant student for role model. Tell student what behavior is desired and what misbehavior is not appropriate. Avoid lecturing. If necessary, move student to back of room and allow student to stand.
The Hostile Student: Student is perpetually angry without apparent cause or provocation. Changes classroom environment. Peers and teacher may feel threatened, angry and frustrated. May refuse to comply with rules, follow routines or do assignments. Wastes time. Causes confusion.	Wants control, power, attention or revenge. Objects to authority and rules. Could be gang or drug involvement. Could be result of abusive relationship. Could be result of repeated social or academic failures.	Do not accept bait. Retain professional, pleasant demeanor while being firm about expectation that class rules and procedures must be adhered to. Affirm student worth with respect and attention. Do not give student the stage. Talk quietly and personally without threatening. Give appropriate options to misbehaviors. Follow through with consequences for misbehavior. Allow student to appropriately express displeasure or complaints. Consider validity of comments. Model appropriateness. Try to be nonjudgmental. Attempt to provide positive opportunities for leadership.

Problem	Possible cause	Possible response
The Apathetic Student: Student shows little or no interest in assignments, discussions or involvement. Does not do or complete work. Doesn't pay attention. Gets poor grades. Has short attention span. Does not seem to have friends. Poor role model for other students. Importance of academic progress is diminished. Teacher may feel frustrated, may ignore student or devote too much time to student, thereby diminishing effectiveness with other students.	May be depressed or feel rejected. May have little self-confidence. Student may feel it easier not to try and fail than to try and fail. May be lacking in academic or social skills. May be bored. May be drug involved. May be poorly nourished and getting inadequate sleep.	Create opportunities for small successes in academic and social settings. Attempt to capitalize on any known interests, talents or skills. Do not lower expectations. Do not call attention to student failure or nonperformance. Try to involve student in learning. Make certain that materials and strategies are appropriate to abilities. Use praise or concrete reward for improved behavior or performance—quietly and personally. Discuss situation with parent, and seek assistance from former teachers or guidance counselor. Continue to show sincere interest and availability to help.
The Defier: Student is highly emotional, exhibits little self-control and talks back. Pushes others to the brink. Student opposes and continually challenges teacher, authority, rules and procedures. Unaffected by what teacher does. May ridicule teacher and refuse to accept consequences of behavior. Tends to blame others or complain about injustices. Peers and students feel threatened and uncertain about how to respond. Student undermines role of teacher while creating tension and interfering with class progress. Rules and discipline are challenged. May cause disquiet and discontent among other students.	Student may be angry at history of inattention or failure. May use defiance as form of protection or survival. May have given up on trying for positive response or success, social or academic.	Calm, professional, caring demeanor is essential. Never debate, threaten or engage in power struggle. Attempt to develop agreement of how student will talk to and behave with others. Don't take defiance personally. Convey that problem is not student but defiance. Make every effort to develop a personal relationship. Attempt to give opportunities for positive roles of power and responsibility. Allow student to express concerns and ask student how to help improve situation. Be specific about what behaviors are inappropriate and require change. Encourage student to become involved in monitoring behavioral change plan.

Adapted from "You Can Handle Them All" website (www.disciplinehelp.com), Stride, 2004.

Power of 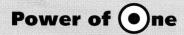ne

The Challenge

As Tyrone White sank into the seat, he released an exasperated sigh and said, "Just what I need today, a few pointers on discipline."

Janice Gold, sitting next to him for the inclusion professional development session on discipline, showed her surprise: "Tom, we all look to you for guidance. You are our discipline guru. We all claim that you lead a charmed life and that your students never misbehave!"

"Well, guess what? Today I need help. Surprisingly, it is not with my students. The discipline problems developing seem to be due to miscommunication and mixed messages with my collaborators."

The Response

Tyrone is certainly not alone in feeling exasperation when discipline problems result not from students but from teachers or paraprofessionals. Tyrone's former experiences and successes should help the team agree on a win-win management scenario for students and staff.

Importantly, Tyrone's situation requires delicate yet forthright immediate action. Obviously communication is poor; without improvement members will not be able to develop effective programs or a productive learning environment. All the professionals and paraprofessionals must confidently present a united front to promote and enforce a proactive discipline plan. That means they need to agree collaboratively on the rules and methods of treatment and possible consequences. Further, it is helpful for team members to establish nonverbal cues for immediate communication with each other to affirm or disaffirm a course of disciplinary action with a student.

SCHOOL DISCIPLINE SURVEY

How does your school stack up when it comes to establishing and maintaining a safe, positive learning environment? Use the following survey to determine the extent to which your school is helping or hindering your classroom management efforts.

	Almost always	Sometimes	Almost never
1. The school is clean, cheerful and orderly in appearance.	☐	☐	☐
2. Staff speak to and treat *all* students respectfully.	☐	☐	☐
3. Staff report to school and classes in a timely fashion.	☐	☐	☐
4. Students report to school in a timely fashion.	☐	☐	☐
5. Staff report to duty assignments in a timely fashion.	☐	☐	☐
6. The disciplinary code is clearly defined and understood by staff, parents and students.	☐	☐	☐
7. Teachers are supported in disciplinary efforts by administration and ancillary staff.	☐	☐	☐
8. School staff work together to maintain discipline.	☐	☐	☐
9. Staff dress and behave in a professional manner.	☐	☐	☐
10. Professional staff presence is obvious between classes and before and after school.	☐	☐	☐
11. Students have a sense of ownership and pride in their school.	☐	☐	☐
13. Staff have a sense of ownership and pride in their school.	☐	☐	☐
14. There is a clearly defined and available chain of command to handle serious disciplinary issues.	☐	☐	☐
15. Administration is readily available to assist staff with emergencies.	☐	☐	☐
16. Administration is readily available to assist students with disciplinary issues.	☐	☐	☐
17. Students and staff feel no threat of violence.	☐	☐	☐
18. The school is free of gang or drug-related incidents.	☐	☐	☐
19. Staff are aware of school, community and parenting resources for supporting students.	☐	☐	☐
20. Effective training for violence de-escalation is provided to staff.	☐	☐	☐
21. Coordinated services and programs for student support and involvement are available and widely known.	☐	☐	☐
22. School teams work on behavioral, social and academic problem solving.	☐	☐	☐
23. Ongoing, effective training provides staff with skills to handle maladaptive behavior.	☐	☐	☐
24. There is a school-wide discipline approach concerning noncompliance, unacceptable behaviors and disruptive behaviors.	☐	☐	☐
25. There is ongoing, meaningful evaluation of instruction, remediation and extracurricular programs as well as staff and administration.	☐	☐	☐

DISCIPLINE PREPAREDNESS SURVEY

Rate yourself. The higher your score, the lower your chances for management problems from your students.

Yes No

☐ ☐ 1. I greet students with a smile. I treat all students respectfully.

☐ ☐ 2. I am purposeful in starting the class, following my objectives and completing work at the end of day.

☐ ☐ 3. I have discussed and posted the class rules.

☐ ☐ 4. I treat offenders proactively, quietly, in a timely manner and with respect.

☐ ☐ 5. Consequences for misbehavior are appropriate to the rule infraction and are prosocial in nature.

☐ ☐ 6. I make an effort to help students avoid rule infractions and self-monitor and self-correct.

☐ ☐ 7. I clearly establish that rules and consequences are in place to ensure a safe environment for learning.

☐ ☐ 8. I role-model respectful behavior and adhere to class rules and standards.

☐ ☐ 9. I make an effort to downplay difficulties and to focus on the academic business of the class.

☐ ☐ 10. I avoid backing angry, upset students into an emotional corner.

☐ ☐ 11. I am open-minded in dealing with student suggestions and complaints and try to act on those having merit.

☐ ☐ 12. I make it obvious that I am there to support and help all students.

☐ ☐ 13. I have established a repertoire of prosocial consequences for inappropriate behaviors.

☐ ☐ 14. I know and have practiced an emergency plan in case of violent behavior.

☐ ☐ 15. I do not hold a grudge. I focus on the positive rather than the negative.

☐ ☐ 16. Students recognize that the class is a safe place and that I deal fairly and firmly with serious infractions.

SUGGESTED ALTERNATIVES TO PUNISHMENT

Consequences for nonviolent rule infraction that have been determined with student involvement have a better chance of positively altering behavior than does the use of punishment. Allowing students some choice allows them some power and possibly the chance to benefit from the consequence. The following alternatives may help as you develop your age-appropriate repertoire of alternatives:

1. Student writes a poem, short story or rap about subject matter or misbehavior.
2. Student prepares and presents a comedy scene showing a positive alternative to misbehavior.
3. Student agrees to attend one after-school session for extra help.
4. Student agrees to attend one school extracurricular function.
5. Student shares with the class a brainteaser, riddle or puzzle or develops a motivating, fun activity related to subject matter being studied.
6. Student agrees to clean up classroom, put books away, file papers, etc.
7. Student draws a picture, develops a graph or creates some other material related to the subject matter to share with the class.
8. Student agrees to sing a selected song in front of the class.
9. Student agrees to assist the teacher in helping another student in a teacher-determined manner or tutor a student after demonstrating mastery of the subject matter.
10. Student brainstorms for three positive alternatives to how the situation might have been handled better.
11. Student devises a self-monitoring procedure and agrees to use it in attempting to positively change behavior.
12. Student agrees to develop a contract with the teacher that focuses on diminishing or eliminating the negative behavior and replacing it with a positive one.
13. Student agrees to write a paragraph explaining why he was the cause of the rule infraction and what he intends to do differently. Student agrees to date and sign it for placement in student's file folder for future reference.
14. Student agrees to brainstorm to develop a list of five ways that the misbehavior impacted negatively on self, peers and teacher.
15. Student agrees to work with the teacher to develop a list of triggers that encourage misbehavior and a personal signal or code to indicate frustration and the need for assistance in averting a potential problem.
16. Student agrees to read a lesson or text assignment on tape for students who are absent or reading disabled.

LIFESTYLE SURVEY

Lifestyle decisions may be the result of family circumstances, habit, choice or unconscious motives. They can impact on relationships and performance. Please take a few moments to respond to the following questions. There is a place to add comments, if you so choose. (Teachers may elect to do this activity as an oral survey for math or science class, especially for younger students. Results can be tabulated and graphed.)

1. About how many hours of TV do you watch daily?

2. About what time do you go to bed?

3. How many hours of sleep do you normally get?

4. How would you describe your energy level during the day?

5. What do you usually eat for breakfast?

6. What do you normally have for lunch?

7. How many glasses of water do you usually drink a day?

8. Who prepares the meals in your home?

9. Who shops for the food?

10. Where do you usually eat dinner?

11. With whom do you usually eat dinner?

12. Are you a junk food freak? If so, what is your preferred junk food and how frequently do you eat junk food?

13. How many servings of fruits and vegetables do you usually have a day?

14. How many hours do you spend on school work daily?

15. Where do you do school work?

16. What type of physical exercise do you do daily?

17. About how long do you exercise daily?

18. What is one thing you feel you should change about your health habits?

Comments: _____

_____

_____

_____

Modifying the Curriculum

WHAT TO DO?

Kara Donnelly and Michelle Elliott had developed a fast friendship since being thrown together as fourth grade inclusion coteachers. They had little time during the school day to talk over concerns or ideas. At the conclusion of each school day, Kara, the general education teacher, and Michelle, the special education teacher, met at the nearby Starbucks to decompress and rehash the day.

Biting into a chocolate muffin and sipping her latte, Kara said in an exasperated tone: "Michelle, wasn't that lesson on reptiles a flop? When I think about the response of the students I get really depressed! Donna had to prove that she knew everything and wouldn't shut up. She insisted on blurting out all the curious facts we planned as hooks for our reading and writing activities and then continually complained how boring the lesson was. I felt like taping her mouth."

"True, but in all honesty, I would have done the same thing that Donna did! I can't stand being 'taught' what I already know inside and out," Michelle responded while sipping her cappuccino. "Did you notice Juan?

He was totally fascinated by the detailed structural pictures, and although he tuned out the lesson, he copied the drawings. (And I have to admit his drawings beat the heck out of any I could do!) And how about Edward? He refused to read aloud, whereas Joanna insisted on reading aloud but couldn't make it through the first paragraph without stumbling so much that no one knew what she was reading."

"Although 'Michelle' had been modifying instruction to meet IEP mandates, more was called for to meet the needs of all students."

Michelle continued in her usual blunt manner. "Yeah, you're right, we bungled that lesson. I think we handled the whole situation poorly, and that set us on the wrong track for the rest of the day. Let's admit it, we're working hard but may not be accomplishing much."

Puzzled, Kara questioned: "What do you mean? What are you talking about? We plan. We know our objectives. We abide by the IEPs. We use visuals. We have interesting information. We don't talk too much. We share instruction. We circulate the room. What more could we do?"

"True, we do those things," Michelle responded, "but we don't really take into account individual differences! Sure, we pay attention to IEPs, but we have other nonclassified kids with similar or worse disabilities. *And,* we have some really talented kids. Their talents are certainly not in the same areas, which means we've got to figure out how to capitalize on them. The disparity in skill level gives us a real challenge. Donna reads at a tenth grade level, Joanna is on a second grade level and Juan is a gifted nonreading artist! Shall I go on?"

bottom line
■ ■ ■ ■ ■ ■ ■ ■ ■ ■

Do what you can, with what your have, where you are.—
David Sarnoff

Frustration and disappointment may be the motivators for Kara and Michelle to begin to differentiate instruction. Although Michelle had been modifying instruction to meet the IEP mandates of the seven identified special needs students in the classroom, more was definitely called for in order to meet the needs of *all* their students.

It's true that elementary teachers are more apt to make efforts to differentiate instruction than are high school teachers. It's also true that those who have focused on students at the fringes have found it essential and rewarding to individualize according to interest, need and ability. Gifted education has long encouraged both horizontal (in-depth) learning and vertical (more advanced) learning. Special education teachers have been trained to assess student needs and adapt instruction, environments and curriculum as appropriate for the student. Yet, for some reason, the general education population is more apt to be subjected to whole class instruction and, as Kara and Michelle had begun to conclude, with less than optimal success.

How is it that we, as teachers, seem to overlook that we each have our own learning styles, preferences and abilities or disabilities that directly impact on the effectiveness of our learning?

Certainly, whole class instruction is less complex and less labor intensive, and may give the teacher a feeling of control as all students are expected to follow the teacher's one pathway to learning. In my opinion, however, one lesson without options is a deceptively easy way out. I call it deceptive because it fails to produce the necessary results expected in this age of accountability, higher standards and public report cards of individual teacher effectiveness.

No two students learn exactly the same way. Students come to class bringing different background experiences, different skills, different needs and different talents. Responsible inclusion presupposes that all students will have access to the curriculum as well as an opportunity to succeed. The reflective, perceptive professional soon realizes that no two students are alike and, consequently, blended instructional alternatives are necessary.

Wrightslaw (wrightslaw.com) reminds us that NCLB legislation impacts on most public education employees. All schools receiving Title 1 federal funds must make annual detailed reports on the progress of special needs students, minority children, children with limited English proficiency and those from low-income families.

Teachers in grades K–3 must teach all children to read using research based methods. Teachers in upper elementary schools must teach reading, math and science at increasingly higher skill levels. Did you know that current research indicates 68% of fourth graders cannot read proficiently at grade level?

bottom line
■ ■ ■ ■ ■ ■ ■ ■ ■ ■

If I treat you as though you are what you are capable of becoming, I help you become that.— *Johann von Goethe*

Behaviors and strategies of effective teachers

Ms. Solomon had taught fifth grade for many years, and although she loved teaching, her students continually performed poorly and were not hesitant to tell anyone, "Ms. Solomon is an old grouch who couldn't teach us anything even if she tried." A short visit to her classroom clearly revealed that although Ms. Solomon was trying desperately to '"cover" the curriculum, the students were out of control, angry and not engaged in learning (at least not the lesson!)

BRIGHT IDEA

Change can be disturbing to students, especially special needs students. Take time, even if briefly, to tell students about upcoming changes and why they will occur. Especially let them know how they personally will benefit from the change.

Effort, knowledge of the subject and a desire to teach are not enough to produce a good teacher.

The following qualities pervade the teaching of the most effective special and general education teachers:

- A pleasant, optimistic attitude coupled with a sincerely demonstrated interest in each individual student.

- Simply stated, clearly defined and enforced rules (often collaboratively developed).

- Safe, orderly learning environment.

- Procedures and routines developed and practiced until virtually automatic.

- Clearly defined instructions modeled with enthusiasm.

- High expectations for behavioral and academic success for all students based on encouragement of self-regulated behavior and learning, but with provision for support and assistance as needed.

- A variety of instructional approaches appropriate to student needs using cues, prompts, guided instruction, encouragement and positive reinforcement.

bottom line

With time and patience the mulberry leaf becomes a silk gown.—*Anonymous*

- Continual monitoring and assessment of student progress toward mastery, with teacher- and self-monitored activities based on those results.

- Multimodal instruction to allow for multiple intelligences with guided practice dependent on need and provided prior to assigning independent practice.

- The ability to enlist students as team members in the learning process.

Assuredly, some effective teachers use differentiated instruction without much conscious effort and, indeed, they may well have gradually transformed their teaching style, methods and materials over the course of their career. Some may not be deliberate in their teaching style. Indeed, if asked, they perhaps would not be able to verbalize the contrast between traditional instruction and their current method of differentiated instruction!

Professional staff development can be invaluable in providing teachers with the tools, strategies and confidence to move toward more differentiated instruction. Bear in mind that if your school receives money under No Child Left Behind, administrators must consult with teaching staff about needs. Ask for help with differentiated instruction! Also, visit the US Department of Education website (www.ed.gov/about/offices/list) or call 1-800-USA-LEARN.

Contrasting traditional and differentiated instruction

It is important to recognize that successful differentiated instruction demands a lot of up-front planning and organizing. I offer the following caveats for your consideration:

- Know why you plan to move away from the traditional methods.

- Start slowly and proceed in accordance with your comfort level and preparedness.

- Apprise and enlist the support of your students and parents, citing your specific reasons for using

bottom line
■ ■ ■ ■ ■ ■ ■ ■ ■ ■

Vision without action is a daydream, action without vision is a nightmare.—
Anonymous

differentiated instruction and how you expect individual student performance to improve.

- If possible, seek out professional staff development help and plan with other colleagues eager to differentiate instruction.

The table on the next page compares and contrasts traditional instruction and differentiated instruction.

"The theory of differentiated learning is accepted by nearly all educators, especially as classrooms become more heterogeneous."

The theory, if not the practice, of differentiated learning is accepted by nearly all educators, especially as classrooms become less homogeneous and more heterogeneous. Unfortunately, many educators do not have the necessary strategies or impetus to make differentiated learning happen. Moreover, a large number indicate they feel overwhelmed and frustrated that they do not know how to proceed (much like most of us who have set a goal to become proficient in some new and challenging area).

Managing diversity of needs

This section is intended to be a how-to guide, answering the questions of the educator interested in moving toward differentiated instruction.

What can be differentiated?

Teachers can begin to differentiate content, process and product in the following manner:

Content   The teacher reflects on and determines the curriculum basics from the essentials to the more advanced aspects of the topic, keeping in mind student differences.

bottom line
■ ■ ■ ■ ■ ■ ■ ■ ■ ■

Ability is what you're capable of doing. Motivation determines what you do. Attitude determines how well you do it.—*Lee Holz*

Process   Using the IEP as the framework, the teacher develops curricular goals for the special needs students, determining the desired outcomes and how to accomplish them. The teacher recognizes the needs of *all* students and offers three or more instructional paths to reach mastery of concepts, with necessary modifications built in for special needs students. This may mean flexible grouping methods such as independent research, partner learning, cooperative or small group learning, large group investigation, or

Traditional	Differentiated
Whole group instruction. Teacher presents lesson in one manner; students are given one means of interacting or responding.	Blends instructional strategies. Provides three or four options for students to learn curricular objectives.
Assessment is used to determine how much of covered material has been mastered or retained, usually at the end of the learning experience.	Requires continual student monitoring and diagnostic assessment to tailor instruction to need.
Student differences are not tapped or utilized.	Engages learners, allowing for individual differences, talents, styles and abilities.
Coverage of instruction is often the teacher's motivator.	Focuses on student differences and multiple intelligences, allowing for more interest based learning.
A single text may dominate.	A variety of resources and materials are provided.
A single form of presenting information is used.	Multiple perspectives and presentation methods are used.
A single form of assessment is used.	Multiple forms of assessment are used.
The teacher is the "sage on the stage."	The teacher works with the students as the "guide on the side."
The teacher manages and directs behavior.	Students are encouraged to self-monitor behavior and work toward self-reliance.
Much large group or whole group work.	A variety of instructional methods are used: independent, study-buddy, small group, cooperative learning, computer-assisted.
Focuses on the average learner.	Allows accommodation for special needs students in order to include the more able and the disabled.
Instruction is grade level and aimed at homogeneous groupings.	Requires considerable ongoing teacher effort and student assessment, recognizing the heterogeneity of the class.

(Adapted from Tomilson, 1999; Stride, 2004.)

multimodal options to access and manipulate information. It may include stations, problem based learning, compacting, agendas, choice boards and so forth. The teacher and students work together in assessing needs, learning styles and interests to develop instructional processes appropriate to students.

Product   The teacher encourages students to demonstrate understanding, skill and mastery through different avenues, such as oral presentation, demonstration, written report, drawings, charts, computer research, multimedia presentations and written or oral exams.

BRIGHT IDEA

Engaging students of different ability levels need not be complicated or expensive, as special educator Dale Hubert found out using an idea developed by Jeff Brown. Each student creates a doll, "Flat Stanley," which comes to life and takes on the student's persona. Students keep a journal of Flat Stanley's experiences and then mail both the doll and the journal to other schools and relatives, in and out of the country. Recipients return Flat Stanley, describing his adventures in the journal and often including pictures from his trip.

Flat Stanley has been a dramatic success with students of all ages around the world, stimulating them to learn about other cultures while enhancing communication and technology skills. For more information go to http://flatstanley.enoreo.on.ca. (Johnston, 2004)

How can differentiation be handled logistically?

Vary the physical environment of the classroom. Allow for flexible arrangements of furniture and students. Establish areas for quiet reflection or independent work, small group work, partner work, computer-assisted work and research. Feel free to change the composition of the groupings and the placement of furnishings to reflect the focus of instruction and the results of ongoing assessment based on student need, interest and learning style. Think of the classroom as a stage for the players (teachers and students).

bottom line

Do not play the blame game. Demonstrate "Where there's a will, there's a way."

How can varied student needs be met?

Individualized instruction and differentiated learning, based on student readiness, interests and learning profiles, depend on regular ongoing assessment and adjustment.

This process may be formal or informal, and written, oral or demonstrated. The stronger the bond between teachers and students, the easier it is to acknowledge differences and preferences as well as the most successful strategies for students.

What instructional and management strategies are available?

The number of instructional and management strategies open to you are limited only by your imagination, determination and energy! Following are strategies used to help differentiate content, process and product. (See the Dictionary of Curriculum Terms at the conclusion of this chapter.)

Pick and choose the ones that fit your teaching style, comfort level and skill level. My advice is to start with a few and gradually add to your repertoire!

- Interest centers
- Taped material and audio books
- Video clips
- Learning contracts
- Tiered lessons, centers, projects, products, assessment
- Varied texts
- Varying organizers
- Compacting
- Varied journal prompts
- Varied homework assignments
- Varied supplemental materials
- Computer-assisted instruction
- Independent learning
- Small group instruction or investigation
- Problem based learning
- Choice boards
- 4MAT
- Orbital instruction
- Reading buddies
- Cooperative learning groups
- Varied rubrics
- Mentors

Adapting curriculum to address behaviors that interfere with learning

Optimal learning occurs best in a safe, orderly environment, presenting the teacher with the onerous challenge of establishing and maintaining a learning environment free of discipline problems. Let's face it—even the most talented, resourceful and compassionate teacher sometimes has to deal with behaviors that interfere with learning. The causes for the challenges are myriad: Immaturity, disability,

bottom line

■ ■ ■ ■ ■ ■ ■ ■ ■ ■

Set the tone for a safe, rigorous and orderly academic environment during the first week.

hostility, irritability due to poor nutrition or inadequate sleep, frustration or desire for attention. Try to ascertain the cause of the problem. Assume that the student would prefer a solution be found to the problem, and proceed accordingly. No matter what the circumstance, I have found it best to handle problem behavior quietly and personally, not to place blame and definitely not to call public attention to any deficiencies. I bet you agree—blame is accusatory and counterproductive.

Handling problematic behaviors of included students

"View your students separate from their behavior; they, too, would prefer to have fewer problems."

Your heterogeneous inclusion class offers you opportunities to work with a very wide spectrum of abilities and behaviors. You are bound to have one or more students who challenge you with "growth possibilities," which at the time you wish you didn't have. In the long run, you'll find that these experiences cause you to stretch professionally and add strategies, skills and materials that will benefit you and your future students. May I remind you to view your students separate from their behavior, especially your special needs students. They may be doing their best to cope with the academic requirements. You can be pretty certain that they, too, would prefer to have fewer problems.

Tempting though it might be, do not expect (or ask) your paraeducator to develop and provide curricular or behavioral modifications. Effective modifications are the responsibility of the trained educator and are the result of considerable thought, planning, resources and communication. Do make every effort to convince students that you (and the rest of the team) are there to facilitate learning and that you will make every effort to help them succeed in overcoming academic or behavioral difficulties.

bottom line
■ ■ ■ ■ ■ ■ ■ ■ ■ ■

Establish high expectations for all. Help the special needs students compensate but do not encourage or permit overcompensation.

The following table lists behaviors rather typical in any classroom, especially the inclusive classroom. I have suggested potential teacher responses to each.

Problem behavior	Possible solutions
Continual interruptions with questions or demands for attention. Student is alerting you to a cognitive or emotional need that requires a quick response. Perhaps the behavior is caused simply by directions or tasks that are not clearly described. If not attended to, the unmet need can lead to frustration and refusal to work, while causing work disruptions impeding the progress of others.	▪ Give one cue at a time. ▪ Ask another student to rephrase a statement. ▪ Keep directions concrete. ▪ Quietly approach student to personally redirect student to the task. ▪ Pantomime instructions or use a puppet to do the reminding or directing.
Difficulty transitioning from one task to another. Student seems unable to efficiently make the necessary change of topic, assignment, location, procedure or routine. Student anxiety may lead to frustration that results in disruptive behavior and certainly the loss of time.	▪ Begin early in the school year to practice transitions from one location to another, one subject to another, one procedure to another. ▪ Demonstrate your expectations. ▪ Build up and practice routines as follows: Forewarn students that a transition will occur soon; remind students about transition; state desired change; request actual transition. ▪ Consider using specific cues that signal a transition is coming, e.g., turn the light on and off a few times to signal only a few minutes remain before . . .
Frequent daydreaming or off-task behavior. Student may be tired, bored, confused or simply uninterested or unable to do the assigned work.	▪ Offer a quiet, redirecting comment (definitely not loudly or directing class attention to the student). ▪ Quietly tap on student's book or paper to draw attention to assignment. ▪ Simply and personally restate topic, sentence or question. ▪ Change student's seat to be near a quiet, good student or close to the teacher's desk. ▪ Move closer to student (within approximately 16–18 inches) to alert student to resume work. ▪ Circulate the room as the lesson progresses to assure on-task behavior. ▪ Give quiet verbal reward for appropriate on-task behavior.

Problem behavior	Possible solutions
Continued lack of involvement in discussions or refusal to respond to direct questions. Student may not understand what is being asked, may not know the answer or may already have fallen into a failure cycle. This may change as trust between you develops.	■ Restate or reword question. ■ Simplify question. ■ Arrange special signal that indicates student's willingness to respond. ■ Encourage student to participate in discussions and answer directed questions. ■ Make brightly colored "bonus point" coupons to award students spontaneously for participation, correct answers or unusually clear and descriptive responses. ■ Allow students to redeem their bonus points for such privileges as being first in line, book monitor, AV specialist for the day.
Refusal to write assigned work or copy notes. This seeming act of defiance may really be an inability to understand expectations, see the notes, write quickly enough or copy correctly. See if you can define which it is.	■ Have student's eyesight checked by the nurse. ■ Move student's desk. ■ Allow student to copy your notes or those of another student. ■ Provide a copy of your notes for student. ■ Keep notes brief, vocabulary as simple as possible and writing legible. ■ Use overhead projector and give student transparency to copy.
Refusal to begin or complete an assignment. Student may not understand what is expected or know how to answer. Student may be overwhelmed with the assignment, particularly tasks requiring written explanations, or not have the appropriate writing implements or resources.	■ Have student restate assigned task. ■ Keep instructions brief and simple. ■ Help student break down assignment into discrete steps and begin work on first step. ■ Have a peer study-buddy discuss question or assignment and suggest ways to go about answering. ■ Help student get started by talking through the beginning of the task and waiting while the student completes that portion. ■ Provide student with preprinted, partially completed notes. ■ Ascertain that appropriate resources are available.

Problem behavior	Possible solutions
Distractibility during written class work or tests. Student may focus on noise or movement in the classroom rather than the assigned work. The student may be confused by the format, spacing or wording of questions in assignments or tests.	■ Redirect student by standing next to student, pointing to question, tapping shoulder gently or quietly calling name. ■ Provide quiet spot or study carrel. ■ Close doors to block outside noise. ■ Reposition student next to quiet, achieving student. ■ Ascertain that student understands expectation. ■ Have student highlight important information. ■ Check whether test modifications are mandated and are being followed appropriately. ■ Use structured study guides for repetition of basic concepts and vocabulary enrichment. ■ Consider practicing sample questions, using similar test format and question construction. ■ Consider allowing students to select from two different formats, with the more difficult one yielding "challenge points."
Difficulty reading or understanding the vocabulary or assignment. Student may have a low reading level or be unfamiliar with the subject-related vocabulary.	■ Preteach vocabulary words, pronunciation and definitions. ■ Assign peer study-buddy to assist in reading. ■ Review directions and vocabulary with student. ■ Have different resources available at less challenging reading level. ■ Use charts, pictures, graphs and tables to convey information. ■ Use tapes and tape recorder for textual assistance. ■ Prepare, or have one of your better readers prepare, tapes of text assignments or notes. ■ Build audio library; have several headsets or iPods available for loan.

Problem behavior	Possible solutions
Continually fails to bring required materials to class. This annoyance to teachers, if not resolved, can spread like wildfire. Ascertain whether the student has the materials (may not be able to afford them, may have lost them, may have stayed overnight at a stepparent's home, etc.), has some other difficulty interfering with bringing them or is intentionally noncompliant.	■ Have student make up work. ■ Have student bring completed work to class the following day. ■ Help student organize notes and notebook to avert problem. ■ Have student suggest appropriate consequence and solution.
Difficulty interacting appropriately or completing group work. Student may have little or no experience working in a group. Student may be unaccustomed to sharing and participating with peers in a small-group learning situation.	■ Clearly identify, teach and practice group work skills and group member roles. ■ Create skill development rubric to be used by group in evaluating member participation. ■ Set clear, narrow guidelines; include demonstration and guided practice. ■ Anticipate, discuss and share solutions to potential group problems. ■ Reward appropriate group work (perhaps give bonus coupons).
Difficulty staying in seat or maintaining appropriate behavior. Student may be diagnosed ADD or ADHD. Could be the result of poor nutrition or poor sleeping habits. Could be unaccustomed to self-discipline and resistant to following directions. Could be anger with something undefined.	■ Seat student away from other distractible students. ■ Consider a contract with student that permits "emergency" leg stretching and a seat in back of room where student may stand or walk without interrupting lesson. ■ Catch student appropriately on task and quietly reward verbally. ■ Consider discussing situation with student and asking for student's assistance and ideas in curbing situation. ■ Check for BIP; talk with guidance counselor or psychologist for suggestions. ■ Attempt to ignore behaviors that are not disruptive. ■ Offer student positive outlet for energy, e.g., being book monitor or audio-visual technician.

Adaped from Stride, 2004.

Power of 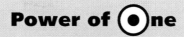ne

The Challenge

Kara admitted to Michelle that it was time to consider how to incorporate differentiated instruction. Fortunately, their mandatory professional development course included sessions devoted to the topic. At the first session, the instructor offered two choices: A written or an oral pretest to determine what each teacher knew about differentiated instruction. Then, using the responses, she organized instruction for the first class. It was obvious that some of the teachers knew terminology, while others had no clue about the terms. Two of the teachers understood the theory but admitted they fell short with implementation. All of them indicated that they needed a KISS (keep it simple, stupid) course.

"Okay," Kara called out, "how do we get started? What are the basics?"

The Response

Michelle was the first to recognize that the instructor was role modeling differentiated instruction. Her first thought was, "Good going—practice what you preach!" It was obvious that their class was first assessed to determine the current level of mastery and need. It was also obvious that the options given were based on the results of assessment.

Because ongoing assessment is critical to differentiated instruction, this seems an easy entry point. Once the teacher recognizes that some students know most of the information, while others know almost nothing about the topic, it becomes obvious what a waste of time and energy it would be to teach the same thing to the entire class.

DICTIONARY OF CURRICULUM TERMS

Academic accommodations   The Committee on Special Education determines if a special needs student requires modifications or accommodations to level the playing field for class work or exams. If so, the specific modification or accommodation will be written into the student's Individualized Educational Plan (IEP). The accommodations may include such things as a scribe, use of a spell checker, directions read, tests read, extended time, use of a calculator or word processor, and perhaps a special location. If accommodations are written into the IEP, they must be granted and provided by all school staff.

Agenda   Individual student plan for activities and tasks to be completed by a specified time. Students may or may not have similar agendas.

Choice board   Posterboard or similar material with many pockets holding color-coded task cards. Students select cards of a particular color (which may reflect different ways to access or respond to curricular tasks).

Compacting   Preassessment of student knowledge and skills allows students to work on alternative learning projects so that able students do not continue on already mastered work.

Complex instruction   The use of more challenging materials and tasks, open-ended questions and probing study with teacher-supported small group work.

Cues   Verbal or visual prompts that provide a hint for the student to recall information.

Differentiated learning   Tiered instruction offers students learning experiences appropriate to individual learning needs. Generally, three or four options or pathways are provided for learning a subject or topic.

Successful differentiated learning   Always begins with assessment. The teacher recognizes that rarely will two students learn alike and that the readiness, learning styles, experiences, talents, skills and interests of students must be considered when presenting content, planning activities, determining the product and making decisions about the learning environment.

Entry points   Students explore a given topic through such different approaches as narration and deductive reasoning. (This term was made popular by Howard Gardner of *multiple intelligence* fame.)

Mnemonic   Memory enhancers or devices used to assist the student to recall facts or ideas. Rhymes (raps), rhythms and music can also be employed as memory tools.

Multimodal instruction   Recognizes that learning styles are as different as ability and motivation levels, and reaches out to learners through different modalities. Teachers may lecture, demonstrate, use a visual, show a video clip, use an audio clip, discuss, use dramatization and employ a variety of work techniques such as independent learning, computer assisted instruction, peer instruction and partner or small group learning.

Orbital instruction So named because it allows a student to focus on independent work that revolves around some aspect of the curriculum being studied. Ideally, students select a topic and teachers guide and support the study.

Problem based learning Students become actively involved in problem solving, such as learning the skills necessary to price carpeting for a new home.

Scaffolded instruction Instructional technique that builds on what students already know to develop confidence and understanding. Master teachers often encourage students to become more independent learners, using these scaffolding techniques:

- Model lesson and then ask that it be performed by the class, a small group or partnership and, finally, an individual.

- Give feedback and promote self-evaluation. Encourage and promote frequent and quick success to avoid a cycle of failure.

- Give ample assistance while teaching new or difficult skills or content; decrease support as students demonstrate mastery.

- Promote independence; diminish dependence.

- Tailor assistance to student needs through cues, modeling, discussing, prompting, etc.

- Know when to say "enough" once mastery has been demonstrated.

Certainly some talented students do not need scaffolding for lesson or skill development. Clearly, intuition, monitoring and assessment will be the guide for providing scaffolding to those students in need and only for those times when they need it.

Scientifically based research The NCLB federal legislation raises the bar for selection of materials, programs and instructional methods to promote academic success for all students. Repeatedly we read that teachers must use research based methods of teaching. Increasingly, federal funds for the purchase of materials, textbooks and programs are limited to those that show scientifically based research and results.

Wrightslaw.com reminds us that the legal definition of scientifically based research is research that "applies rigorous, systematic, and objective procedures to obtain valid knowledge . . . and employs systematic, empirical methods that draw on observation or experiment, rigorous data analyses and has been accepted by a peer-reviewed journal or approved by a panel of independent experts through a comparably rigorous, objective, and scientific review."

Standards based learning   Instruction and evaluation of student mastery are referenced to clearly established standards. The intent of standards based instruction is to improve the performance of students so that they can better compete in a global marketplace.

The Master Teacher on PARENTScount.net informs us that standards based learning is not all that new. By 1998 forty-nine states had adopted educational standards in an effort to establish student learning goals and teacher accountability for student success in reaching them. Nonetheless, it is probably fair to say that many teachers and parents do not have a clear understanding of their state's educational standards and progress toward them.

Check out Quality Counts 2005 website (http://www.edweek.org/qc05), sponsored by Education Week, for an annual report on the state of our nation's schools. The report includes an executive summary, state report cards, state data tables and other important state educational information. [WEB ADDRESS NOT VALID]

Stations   Teachers set up a variety of learning environments where students can work on different assignments using different materials and methods.

Strategy instruction   The NCLB legislation has refocused educators' attention on tools, plans and methods that increase student learning or improve social skills. For many years, certain strategies (cues, outlining, highlighting, questioning, mapping, visualization, self-monitoring, mnemonic devices, etc.) have proven effective in improving the learning of special needs students. The increased pressure for schools, teachers and students to meet higher proficiency standards has driven the use of strategy instruction into the mainstream to raise the performance levels of all students.

Strategic learners   Students who have had deliberate instruction in cognitive strategies and have mastered these strategies tend to be more responsible and confident in their learning ability. They are reported to be able to recognize more than one way to learn and begin to develop a personal study and work process.

Tiered instruction   Lessons are constructed so that the core instructional objectives are met using different avenues for learning and demonstration of mastery, enabling the more able and the less able to be engaged in the learning process.

For example: A science lesson on the earth's structure may have an introductory minipresentation by the teacher introducing key concepts and vocabulary, followed by exploratory options. These might include independent or small group in-depth research using primary resources or Internet searching, exploration using an audio book with visuals, or a traditional textbook assignment involving reading and responding to questions. Demonstration of mastery might involve a multimedia presentation, an oral report, a drawing explained by a written summary or perhaps an oral discussion with opportunities for question and answers.

Self–regulation   Students are taught how to monitor and regulate their own learning and behavior. They learn to take responsibility for doing things on their own when possible, for performing routines without reminders and for using learning strategies that have been taught. This independence in learning is self-motivating and time saving while promoting responsibility for personal success.

Transitions   Transitions involve changes in place, time, subject, routine or procedures. Effective teachers learn many tools to optimize transitions to save time, enhance learning, refocus attention, encourage on-task behavior and provide for positive energy release, thereby reducing behavioral problems. An encouraging outgrowth of productive transitioning is consideration for the rights of others and the responsibility to respect those rights.

4MAT   Teachers break down a given topic into four learning preferences to allow students to approach the topic in a variety of modes to enhance learning.

(Adapted from Tomlinson, 1999.)

ACADEMIC SUCCESS SURVEY

This self-survey can be quickly administered to students during the opening weeks of school as part of a focus activity or closing activity. (It can be read orally and filled in by individual students.) Results for the group (not individuals) could be shared and discussed with the class to generate suggestions on how to modify instruction to maximize strengths and compensate for weaknesses.

Preferably, arrange individual conferences with interested students to discuss personal strengths and weaknesses. Encourage students to suggest personal options; subsequently, discuss other available options for assistance or compensation.

We all have learning strengths and weaknesses. Write an "E" in front of those areas below that are easy for you. Write a "D" in front of those areas that are difficult for you.

_____ Speaking up in class; participating in class discussions
_____ Volunteering an answer
_____ Reading out loud
_____ Reading silently
_____ Finding the main ideas
_____ Outlining
_____ Maintaining an organized notebook
_____ Taking notes or copying notes accurately
_____ Performing mathematical computation
_____ Graphing
_____ Studying for tests
_____ Remembering facts
_____ Taking tests
_____ Working independently
_____ Staying on task, completing work
_____ Working with a partner or in a small group
_____ Writing complete sentences or paragraphs
_____ Staying focused
_____ Remembering material presented orally
_____ Recalling information you have read
_____ Making an oral presentation
_____ Following directions
_____ Learning from demonstrations
_____ Doing independent research
_____ Using appropriate language
_____ Reading and recalling subject area vocabulary

Other strengths or difficulties that I have: _____

_____

IMPROVING STUDENT FOCUS CHECKLIST

Many of today's children have irregular eating and sleeping habits as well as uncertain study habits, making it difficult for them to maintain attention to academic work. The following may help you maintain their focus.

Check each technique that you have tried and found successful:

- ☐ Using videodisc for audio/visual subject matter presentation.
- ☐ Using audiotape or video clips to enhance lessons.
- ☐ Using large, colorful, interesting visuals; computer graphics; videos; overheads; tables; graphs.
- ☐ Using student name in questioning or affirming an answer.
- ☐ Dividing class period into segments that are multimodal; reducing teacher talk time.
- ☐ Using team games for review and test preparation.
- ☐ Using student-conducted review and student-constructed questions to review for test. Allowing students to present special projects or make videos or tapes to help others.
- ☐ Giving concrete, simple directions.
- ☐ Reducing extraneous classroom audio and visual stimuli. Using bulletin boards for current topics; removing old displays.
- ☐ Speaking in a soft voice. Varying your tone and inflection. Varying tempo of lesson. Using humor.
- ☐ Developing "specials"—short lessons or units of high interest with varied activities.
- ☐ Reinforcing the importance of accuracy over speed.
- ☐ Preteaching unit or lesson. Having students brainstorm vocabulary and concepts they feel relevant. Giving a pretest to determine appropriate follow-up activity.
- ☐ Encouraging and checking note taking and notebook organization.
- ☐ Giving positive encouragement. Rephrasing answers and acknowledging students for appropriate answers.
- ☐ Pausing after asking questions, allowing students to reflect before answering.
- ☐ Modeling appropriate forms and assignment completion. If possible, showing samples.
- ☐ Being open to student questions, ideas and criticism.
- ☐ Using flash cards, charts, tables and graphs to review major concepts.
- ☐ Using interactive note packets. Completing portions. Filling in answers on overhead to ensure accuracy.
- ☐ Using rhyme, rap, song and mnemonics to assist in fact retention.
- ☐ Making extra credit projects available to extend learning or improve grades.
- ☐ Making extra help easily accessible and available on a regular basis.
- ☐ Experimenting with level of lighting (may be too bright or too dark.)
- ☐ Experimenting with seating arrangements. Avoiding long-term permanent seats. Telling students that seats will be changed regularly (giving you latitude to change as necessary).

8

Assessing Inclusion Students

THE STRESS MESS

Cooling down from their afternoon "let off steam" jog around the school track, Rick turned to his running partner and said: "Let me tell you something, Tony. I have about had it! Not only is this my first year of inclusion teaching, it's my first year of trying to work with coteachers to develop and implement an appropriate and fair grading system. And here it is almost report card time and we are still unable to reach agreement. As if that's not enough, I had a note in my mailbox from the assistant principal informing me that she is coming in to observe tomorrow."

Tony, with sarcasm, responded: "Nice. I'm sure that made your day. Yep, the stress mess! All the BS about cutting back on the paperwork and increasing support for teachers—we get lots of talk but not much action."

Rick, picking up the thread of the complaint, continued: "As long as we're griping, let me tell you what really ticks me off. Our inclusion team has been thrown together in a sink or swim manner with no guidelines. We have tried to develop a collaborating style that benefits the students. The administration neglects to give us shared planning time, they provide no effective staff development, they beat us to death with the dual mantras of 'raise standards' and 'differentiate the learning,' and *then* they have the nerve to call us in and threaten us about failure rates. In the past ten years, there has never been any evaluation of inclusion. Don't they want to know what is working and what isn't?"

Tony elected to add his complaints: "What kind of deal is that? We get warned about accountability—to the state, to the community, to the students. Trust me, I am not thrilled with the idea of class report cards being published on the district website and in the papers. Give me a break!"

"Your inclusion team can move toward more effective in-class evaluations that will help you, your students and parents."

While pulling off his running shoes, Rick turned to Tony and responded: "Well, tomorrow should be interesting. I have not been told the purpose or focus of the observation, nor the criteria. Will this observation really be considered an evaluation? Is it another 'gotcha' opportunity, or will there be some constructive assistance and criticism offered? Perhaps I should consider it a subtle reminder of how we sometimes assess student progress!"

If you are one of the many teachers looking for the magic bullet that will end the confusion and anxiety about evaluation and grading in your inclusion class, I'm afraid you will have to keep looking. The fact is that you are bound by decisions made by others: The federal government, the state, the school district and the school. Your grading system must work in concert with their guidelines as far as report cards are concerned. But all is not lost! This chapter will offer some hints on how your inclusion team can move toward more purposeful, effective and meaningful in-class evaluations that will help you, your students and parents or guardians.

bottom line
■ ■ ■ ■ ■ ■ ■ ■ ■ ■

Courage is not the towering oak that sees storms come and go; it is the fragile blossom that opens in the snow.—*Alice Mackenzie Swaim*

And you, the elementary school teacher, has, in my opinion, one of those challenging, stimulating and stressful jobs our society depends on. Perhaps at no other time in our history has successful teaching performance been so critical. A confluence of issues makes yours a more daunting task than ever:

- The inclusion of the disabled in general education with little or no preparation for staff or students.

- An increasingly well-educated global student body competing with the American student for advanced educational and employment opportunities.

- Continued outsourcing by American corporations looking for a cheaper and better prepared labor source.

- A growing number of ESL students.

- The demand for and publication of reports about student and school progress in newspapers and on websites.

If you think your job is not of vital importance, read on! Carneval and Desrochers (2004), in a summer professional development seminar, stated: "Educators have cultural and political missions to ensure there is an educated citizenry to continue to defend and promote America's democratic ideals. . . . the inescapable reality is that ours is a society based on individual economic autonomy. Those who are not equipped with the knowledge and skills necessary to get, and keep, good jobs are denied full social inclusion and tend to drop out of the mainstream culture, polity, and economy."

- A push for a more rigorous curriculum and higher standards, with more frequent high stakes exams.

- A parent body that is frequently not available to assist and support their children or the school.

The important news is that you have elected to teach. Never underestimate your influence, probably second only to the family in nurturing, guiding and inspiring our children to grow and succeed academically and behaviorally. Evaluation (or assessment) and grading are critical issues for tracking growth, especially when teachers and schools are being held directly responsible for student academic success or failure.

Why assess?

Ah, a good question, and a contentious one. Detractors of assessment are legion, offering reasons such as these:

bottom line
∎ ∎ ∎ ∎ ∎ ∎ ∎ ∎ ∎ ∎

Students who feel they have a chance to pass are more likely to be motivated to participate.

- "We test our students to death."

- "Our teachers only teach to the test; real learning is lost!"

- "What are we really gaining by spending so much time and money on assessment?"

- "They assess to put the onus on the teachers, as if the result of persistent demands for continued high stakes assessment will result in improved teaching and learning."

- "Test results are not a real indicator of progress since we do not use value added testing."

- "Minorities and the disabled get the short end of the stick."

BRIGHT IDEA

Assessment need not be formal. Indeed, daily informal assessment, including visual check-ups, can provide valuable information to help you determine a student's understanding and ability to perform to established standards. Further, it enables you to plan appropriate intervention programs, track progress, diagnose weaknesses, recognize strengths and, most importantly, better prepare your materials, presentations and techniques to meet the needs of students.

I'm sure you have heard or felt some of these sentiments at some point in your career. I'm sure you also know a few teachers who put little thought into the grading process and have gotten away with little attention to valid assessment. Hopefully, the following story will not remind you of one of your own not-so-professional colleagues.

bottom line

Just because you give a test does not mean you have accurately and fairly assessed student knowledge and performance.

Mr. D exemplified the "don't sweat it" approach. Mr. D's grades were much like a hand-crafted quilt, personally designed abstractions, embroidered with As and Bs. His approach was to pacify the students and the parents, keeping them happy with inflated grades. Paper and pen tests were the extent of his assessment repertoire. Mr. D's tests had little content validity, and if the students did poorly, he discounted questions and assigned grades on a curve. Consequently, students did not feel obliged to listen, to strive, or to study because everything they did not only was acceptable, it was superlative. His apparent philosophy: "So what if there is little reflection of fact or reflection of performance level?" (Does that make your blood boil as much as it makes mine? Let's not ask why Mr. D is permitted to continue to "teach"; that is an issue for another book!) Let's not focus on the Mr. D's in education, but rather on professionals like you, eager to use assessment as a tool, eager to find ways to help *all* of your students progress academically and behaviorally.

The why of assessment boils down to the simple truth that if you don't know where your students are academically, you have no way of determining if they are making progress. You also have no way of knowing if your inclusion teaching is effective, which for professionals is reason enough to assess regularly!

BRIGHT IDEA

The precursor to evaluation is trust. When students feel confident that the evaluator uses her results as a tool to promote student progress in process and product, anxiety is diminished.

Begin early in the school year to establish a shared commitment to growth based on valid and constructive assessment of progress. Take time to involve parents in your intents, your tools and your methods. Encourage students to self-assess and to use results in their efforts to improve. Do not use assessment as a threat. Avoid "gotcha's."

What to assess

Perhaps from previous chapters you have realized that I am a firm believer in ongoing constructive evaluation that includes assessment of the following:

- Yourself and your instructional techniques.

- The inclusion team's collaborative relationship and their relationship with students; the inclusion team's collaborative coordinated teaching effectiveness.

- The classroom environment.

- The alignment of instructional objectives and activities to state curricular standards.

- The relevancy, rigor and appropriateness of materials.

- The success of all students in grasping and mastering the subject matter.

bottom line
■ ■ ■ ■ ■ ■ ■ ■ ■ ■

Most included students want the same texts, activities, tests, grading policy and treatment as their mainstream peers.

Maximizing effectiveness of the school report card

You and your inclusion collaborators may feel that the currently used school report card is not appropriate for accurately conveying important information about your students, especially considering the wide range of abilities and disabilities. No point focusing on what you cannot change. *Focus on the fact that the school-wide reporting system is based on your internal classroom assessment process.* Further, by providing and communicating the results of daily and weekly assessments, they will yield much information that you and your team members can use to make the best of the established reporting system.

Using multiple assessment tools

In previous chapters, the need for multimodal teaching has been explored and encouraged to maximize the learning of all students. Certainly, inclusion increases student diversity. Diversity of students implies the need for diversity of instructional techniques as well as the need for diversity of assessment techniques. As you and your team members consider how best to assess the progress and performance of all, bear in mind that the use of multiple assessment tools provides more comprehensive and accurate information about all types of learners, especially those with special needs. I suspect that you will discover previously hidden assets in your students, especially the low-performing students, as you devise and implement multiple assessment techniques. I also suspect that you will avert some of the concerns of the inclusion team about the fairness of the evaluation process for all students, including special needs students.

bottom line
■ ■ ■ ■ ■ ■ ■ ■ ■ ■

Many students benefit from a grading policy dependent on multiple assessment criteria.

For your consideration, the following table offers a smorgasbord of evaluation practices. Pick and choose those you feel appropriate to your situation. It is my hope that you will be inspired to use several alternatives that will provide your team with important information to tailor teaching and student learning, in addition to broadening your approach to grading.

Assessment	Description	Critique
Quiz	Short, formal or informal, oral or written, evaluation of specific subject matter. (Can be multiple choice, fill in the blank, true/false or short answer.)	■ Easily constructed. ■ Allows for quick review of main ideas. ■ Yields superficial and sketchy view of mastery of specific subject matter.
Pass/fail	Student either can or cannot respond correctly.	■ Very general and can be misleading. ■ Yields little constructive information about specific strengths or deficits. ■ Can be discouraging to student who fails and makes passing student overconfident.
Narrative	Teacher reviews student progress, product or process and then provides a written explanation and evaluation, preferably with substantiation to objectify comments.	■ Subjective comments can be disputed unless specific criteria have been determined. ■ Difficult to quantify and objectify without a rubric in place prior to writing narrative.
Progress checklist	Teacher (possibly with student input) constructs a developmental ladder of incremental progress. Teacher uses a commercially established checklist that corresponds to course objectives or behavioral goals. Teacher (and/or student) places a check mark to indicate present level of performance or progress.	■ Teacher (and student) must develop a baseline as a reference point from which to monitor growth. ■ Essential to develop appropriate benchmarks or goals. ■ Feedback to students and parents can be detailed and specific. ■ Yields critical information on progress toward mastery and identifies deficiencies still to be overcome.

Assessment	Description	Critique
Number or letter grades	Typical and widely used percentage grade or letters given to reflect level of performance or proficiency. Generally A, B, C, D, F, but sometimes E for excellence, G for good, F for fair, U for unsatisfactory.	■ Quick. ■ Yields little critical information regarding strengths, deficits or progress. ■ Subjective. ■ Rewards able student. ■ Does not identify areas for improvement. ■ Often an expectation by students and parents.
Performance based assessment	Teacher develops a demonstrable scale to determine student progress or proficiency at completing a specific task or demonstrating knowledge. (Preferably developed with student input and with desired performance demonstrated prior to assessment.) Can be formal when student knows the assessment is taking place. Can be informal when teacher observes student who is uninformed about assessment.	■ Informal performance assessment can be a quick and easy way to determine level of student performance and how much support is necessary. ■ Formal can be helpful because both teacher and student benefit from specific information about performance level. ■ Easily shared with parents. ■ Can be time consuming to determine criteria and to administer individually. ■ Good tool for poor traditional test takers.

Assessment	Description	Critique
Rubrics	A rating scale or scoring guide devised to objectively measure student mastery on given topic or assignment. Rubrics can be developed by teacher alone or with students. Definite performance criteria are developed and shared prior to use. Holistic and analytic rubrics are used. (See Guidelines for Holistic Rubric Design at end of chapter.)	▪ Helps students work toward a higher standard by defining clear expectations, especially if students are coauthors of the rubric. ▪ Can be time consuming and difficult to develop appropriate criteria that correspond to curricular objectives. ▪ Yields in-depth information for teacher, students and parents. ▪ Can be used across a variety of formats: Individual or group work, written, visual, multimedia, etc.
Group activity	Work partners are selected by students or assigned by teacher for a specific purpose. Work is to be completed in the group to fulfill given requirements. Students may be given multiple resources, multiple means of expression and presentation and multiple means of assessment.	▪ Can be time consuming and difficult to assess individual vs. group contributions and to establish individual and group expectations. ▪ Objective individual assessment is difficult. ▪ Allows for interpersonal development and acceptance of a variety of abilities. ▪ Can encourage individual growth toward responsible group effort. ▪ Can accommodate needs and skills of diverse learners. ▪ Requires diligent teacher preparation, observation and guidance.

Assessment	Description	Critique
Student demonstrations or student taught lessons	Student is given the opportunity to prepare and present a lesson on a topic of student's or teacher's choosing. Demonstration may be multimodal but should meet predetermined objectives.	▪ Risky but can be especially rewarding for the presenter. ▪ Student must really know topic. ▪ Time consuming. ▪ Teacher assistance required for all steps: Researching, preparing, presenting and assessing quality of demonstration. ▪ Objective assessment involves aspects of preparation, delivery and presentation. ▪ A suitable rubric is best established prior to presentation. ▪ Not appropriate for reporting broad subject matter mastery.
Self-assessment	Student assesses own process or product based on predetermined criteria. Student, teacher or both may design rubric or checklist.	▪ Encourages student involvement and investment in assessment as a learning tool. ▪ Objectivity and reliability are questionable without a preset rubric. ▪ Reduces student anxiety about assessment of performance or product while refocusing student on criteria for meeting predetermined standards.

Assessment	Description	Critique
Portfolios	A collection of student work that is representative of effort, progress and progress in a specific area. Portfolio materials can be teacher selected, student collected or collaboratively collected.	▪ Allows a value added approach to viewing a student's progress. ▪ Time consuming. ▪ Should be a collection that is viewed in entirety. ▪ Requires storage space. ▪ Does not allow for precise measurement. ▪ Difficult for formal and objective assessment. ▪ Allows feedback to students and parents about strengths and deficits in relation to growth.
Contracts	Teacher and student develop a learning contract setting forth definite objectives, dates for check-in and completion, and expectations for demonstrating mastery. Can be behavioral or academic and based on need or interest.	▪ Encourages independent growth. ▪ Requires the guidance and support of the teacher throughout the contract. ▪ Allows for review, informal assessment and encouragement as student meets with teacher for check-in along the way to completion. ▪ Helpful for those special needs students requiring growth toward independence yet needing short-term reinforcement and support to complete work.

Assessment	Description	Critique
Curriculum based assessment	A tool for assessing content based objectives such as rules, skills and procedures. Often professionally designed and associated with a given text.	■ Helpful in assessing product and process but not progress unless done regularly. ■ Better for rote evaluation than in-depth concept evaluation. ■ Often yields a small picture of performance related to the overall curriculum. ■ Often professionally prepared, making administration and grading fairly easy.
Progress monitoring	The current level of performance is determined and student academic (or behavioral) performance is measured daily or weekly to track progress. Instructional materials and techniques are adjusted accordingly. This relatively new term is sometimes used interchangeably (and not necessarily accurately) with Curricular Based Measurement or Assessment. The US Office of Special Education reminds us that it should be scientifically based and supported by significant research.	■ The yield can be great for providing information for efficient and appropriate instruction, setting higher standards for teaching and making more informed decisions. ■ Difficult for the untrained to implement without support.

Assessment	Description	Critique
Alternate assessment	Alternate assessment is a type of assessment used for some special needs students in situations where standard formal assessment is deemed inappropriate, even with accommodations. Not to be confused with alternative assessment (any method other than the typical paper and pen type, as listed in this table). For more information, check www. education.umn.edu/ [Search *alternative assessments*]	■ NCLB limits the use of alternate assessment to only those students most significantly cognitively impaired. ■ The IEP team, not the classroom teacher, determines student eligibility for this type of assessment. ■ Alternate assessment is expected to relate to the general curriculum. ■ No single model exists and there is much confusion and concern about appropriate construction.
Interview	Teacher and student sit down and talk about how student views progress, strengths and weaknesses. The student is encouraged to discuss alternative ways of accessing and demonstrating knowledge.	■ Time consuming. ■ Requires teacher to consider guidelines for discussion. ■ Builds student-teacher bond and strengthens the notion of teamwork in learning. ■ Informal and subjective assessment. ■ Will require tact and substantiation on part of teacher to offer constructive criticism.
Observation	Teacher routinely observes student behaviors and performance.	■ Informal. ■ Generally subjective. ■ Can be ongoing. ■ Efficient use of time. ■ Helpful in continually aligning instruction to needs. ■ Helpful in alerting teacher to deficits in skill or comprehension in order to design intervention strategies.

LEGAL ALERT

Although the US Department of Education has not yet permitted states to use the value added model to meet the NCLB mandates related to adequate yearly progress, some states are participating in a value added experimental project, perhaps in anticipation of a change in point of view. (Olson, 2004)

If you are new to teaching or to inclusion coteaching, do not be overwhelmed by the wide variety of optional tools available to you. Notice the word *optional!* Options infer choice and that is exactly what I suggest. Select methods and tools that work for you, your coteachers, your students and your situation. May I suggest that you and your collaborating team members review options, reflect and perhaps experiment to find the options most appropriate to meet all needs, including those of the special needs students.

Value added methods

Many professionals express dismay and alarm that they are being held accountable for previous teacher and student failures, asserting that they accept students at varying academic levels and are expected to move them forward from that point to meet the current year's higher standards. This concern has led to much discussion of what is referred to as a "value added" method, in which the effectiveness of schools and teachers is determined by the amount of progress a student makes from one year to the next. As you might imagine, there are many cheerleaders for such a method, but the question of whether it is a more fair method remains to be proven.

bottom line
■ ■ ■ ■ ■ ■ ■ ■ ■ ■

Homework should be treated as a formative assessment of student work and used to prepare students to earn good grades.

We all have seen significant changes in the educational environment with the advances of technology. Today it may seem that this value added concept is too difficult to track—perhaps so, perhaps not. Consider that the NCLB law mandates that states test every student annually in reading and mathematics in grades 3–8. It does not take much imagination to envision a time not too far off when tracking individual student progress from year to year will be a certainty. Schools are judged on the number of students who perform at proficient levels. Therefore, schools that have done a remarkable job advancing students may still be penalized because, in spite of progress, students are not performing at a proficient level. Consequently, those schools may well wish for acceptance of value added assessment.

"With the 'value added' method, the schools' effectiveness is determined by the students' progress from one year to the next."

If value added seems like a no-brainer and you are asking why anyone would oppose such a concept, consider this. If this method were used consistently, it would be fairly easy to establish whether a teacher is continually effective, average or ineffective. Not all educators are willing or eager to have such results known! Enough said.

Coming soon to your school— formative assessment?

Testing and assessment is a field ripe for innovation and moneymaking! The publishing industry is rapidly moving to capitalize on the push for educators to align teaching with state curricular standards. Indeed, the formative assessment market is one of the fastest growing aspects of test publication. But why? Well, one important reason for the increased interest and growth of this market is quite simple. Teachers do want to improve teaching and student performance; however, the stress of devising assessments that measure student performance according to the new rigorous standards is great. Not many have the time, energy or proficiency to tackle the job on their own.

So publishers have found a new, lucrative niche. They have begun to provide online data management software that allows teachers to select items related to grade level, subject, content standards and degree of difficulty. Teachers may then construct their own tests or have the software produce the test. Further, the software will provide item analysis, track performance by standard, score the exams and suggest specific interventions. With many school districts already concerned about finances, a cost of approximately $9 per student may make such services prohibitive.

bottom line
■ ■ ■ ■ ■ ■ ■ ■ ■ ■

Students and parents are entitled to fair, accurate and objective evaluation criteria and procedures.

bottom line
■■■■■■■■■■■

Assessment of students allows the reflective teacher to self-assess style and professional performance.

Final thoughts on assessment

Like it or not, if you are an educator you will be involved in assessment. As with most things, the more you know about the topic, the better off you and your students will be. In this case, if you, the educator, are knowledgeable about and willing to use multiple assessment tools and techniques, you will help improve the opportunities for student success and growth. As a result, you will also improve your own "report card." That can be quite a motivating factor in itself!

Power of ⊙ne

The Challenge

Sharon Brown "inherited" her entire fifth grade class from Mr. D. The class was promoted intact and arrived expecting that they would continue to receive all As and Bs on their report cards. Ms. Brown's students were surprised and angry when tests were returned with comments, suggestions and even poor grades. The school's policy mandated sending home interim reports to apprise parents of performance and progress. Sharon worked conscientiously to evaluate and report, as accurately as possible, the current academic performance of the students. Parental response was not what she had hoped for. It was only a few hours after students arrived home when Sharon began receiving phone calls from angry, upset parents. Hurt, confused and confounded by parental uproar, Sharon really did not know how to respond.

The Response

Sharon definitely is in a dilemma. Assuredly, Mr. D should be the recipient of the parental anger and negativity caused by his deceitfulness. But the blame game never works. What's past is past.

Here's another situation that underscores the importance of the "likability" factor. If Sharon's students like her and begin to trust her, she's half way there. If students feel her real concern for their growth and her desire to involve them in the learning and assessment process, they will undoubtedly convey this to parents. In the meantime, while awaiting the student spillover, Sharon will benefit by regularly communicating information related to curricular standards, activities and expectations. Further, Sharon should invite parents to share their questions, comments and, certainly, their assistance in helping their children grow. If she is using web posting of assignments, as well as weekly parent emails, parents will respond to her efforts more positively and quickly.

DOS AND DON'TS
FOR INCLUSION GRADING

Do	Don't
Offer mandated testing modifications in the least intrusive and obtrusive manner possible.	Call attention to those students in need of testing modifications.
Give positive feedback when possible. For example: "Great job on the writing part of the test. You gave four important facts."	Post grades or read grades aloud.
Encourage oral presentations (formal or informal).	Penalize the unsure or quiet student who prefers not to or refuses to participate.
Use multiple assessment techniques.	Use only one measure for determining grades.
Encourage creative ways to demonstrate mastery.	Expect all students to perform well on pencil and paper tests.
Give several shorter or less extensive tests more frequently.	Give one long, intensive and extensive test.
Grade papers yourself or have students grade their own papers.	Have students grade another's work.
Grade notebooks or folders for completion and neatness.	Fail to expect that notebooks be kept up-to-date.
Include bonus questions for all and challenge questions for those more able.	Give tests constructed at a single level of challenge.
Consider a fun question to reduce test-taking stress.	Administer handwritten or poorly formatted exams.
Review before the test day. Construct tests from study outlines of concepts and terms.	Use tests made by peers that do not reflect your teaching.
Answer subject matter questions prior to disbursing tests.	Introduce any new material on test day.
Use tests as teaching tools for unit or high stakes exams.	Use grades as threats.
Allow for retake of test in an alternate format. Allow students to correct and resubmit test items. Consider giving partial credit for corrected items.	Use tests as an end rather than a means to improve learning.

Do	Don't
Give an open notebook or take home test.	Make personal negative comments about grades or test scores.
Allow students to practice devising test items and answering them.	Give unclear directions on tests or imprecise information about grading policy.
Allow time to practice using new test formats prior to the testing day.	Make tests cumbersome and confusing as to how or where to answer questions; require students to transfer information from one paper to another.
Maintain a quiet, nonthreatening testing environment.	Talk or allow others to talk during testing.
Accept and encourage critical suggestions about grading techniques and policy from students and parents.	Be rigid, positional or defensive about grading techniques and policy.
Provide opportunities for small group work, e.g., everyone brainstorms a problem, one records, one reports to the class.	Rely on individual work.

STUDY SKILL TIPS
FOR UPPER ELEMENTARY STUDENTS

Grades can be improved. Scores on tests can go up. Test taking stress can be reduced. Try the following and chart your progress!

1. Organize your notebook into sections. Always date your notes and put them in order (most recent either in the front or in the back of the section).

2. Listen carefully during class. Ask questions any time you don't understand something.

3. Take complete notes. Keep study guides or photocopies handed out by your teachers. If you are absent, get and copy the notes from a good student or the teacher.

4. Spend the first moments of each class reviewing previous notes. Develop a habit of daily rereading your notes from class. Plan ahead. Set aside time over the weekend to review the week's notes, vocabulary and main concepts.

5. Jot down new vocabulary words and terms. Keep a special section with subject area terms. Include meanings.

6. Use a highlighter. Highlight only the *most* important information.

7. Make flashcards for vocabulary words and/or main concepts. Study them whenever you have a few free minutes (on the school bus, in waiting rooms, etc.).

8. During study time before an exam, make a checklist of important things you should know. Cross them off the list as you study them.

9. Get in the habit of jotting down questions you want answered by your teacher. Write down questions you think might be on a test; be sure you can answer them.

10. Think about a study buddy, but only if the person is serious about learning. Establish a time for study and goals for what you intend to cover. Do not waste time or talk about nonstudy topics. Work together on a regular basis to review notes, vocabulary, concepts and worksheets. If you find that time with your study buddy is not productive, discontinue it and study on your own.

11. For textbook assignments: Pre-read textbook readings by scanning the assignment, looking at the pictures and reading the captions. Use a 3 x 5 inch card held directly below your reading place to focus attention on the selected passage. Look at all the topic headings. Read any questions at the end of the assigned material. Ask yourself "What is this chapter trying to say?" Read the chapter with a questioning mind, looking for who, what, when, where, why and how. Reread and try to summarize the main topics in your own words. Make flash cards or take notes of vocabulary and important concepts.

12. Study at the same time and place daily. Develop the habit.

STRATEGIES FOR HIGH STAKES TEST TAKING
FOR UPPER ELEMENTARY STUDENTS

- Do *not* talk to others about the test on the day of the test. Clear your desk except for the required tools (pen, pencil, highlighter, ruler, calculator, etc.)
- Listen carefully to instructions. Read them carefully. Highlight what you must do to answer the question. Highlight choices or vocabulary that can help you in your answer.
- Note how much time you have. Scan the test format and the point structure for each section. Decide how you can best use your time to get the most points.
- Before you begin, write down any memorized study hints, formulas and facts in the margins.
- Look through the test and highlight terms or ideas that might help you.
- Do not spend time on a question about which you are unsure. Circle it or make a notation in the margin and return to it later. You may recognize the answer in another question.
- After you have finished, go back over the entire test to make sure you have answered every question.

Multiple choice tests

- If two answers are similar, pick the one you feel is best. Avoid answers with phrases including *always* or *never*.
- Select an answer that uses grammar correctly.
- Place answers in the correct location on "bubble sheets" or answer sheets.
- Read the question and answer it in your own words before looking at the choices. Find the answer that corresponds.
- If you have to guess from a wide range of numbers, pick one in the middle.
- Try to eliminate two choices. Select the best remaining answer.

Tests with written responses

- Highlight or underline exactly what is asked of you. If there are several parts to the question, number them so you answer all parts.
- Highlight verbs that tell what you are to do. If you are to compare items, do not list; if you are to describe, do not compare.
- Make a brief outline *before* beginning to write your answer in sentence form.
- Make certain you give key concepts and enough information to answer the question.
- Get to the point. Consider using the wording of the question in your answer.

GUIDELINES FOR HOLISTIC RUBRIC DESIGN

The more effective your rubric (rating scale), the more effective the evaluation of student work (process or product). There are two types of rubrics: Holistic and analytic.

A holistic rubric considers the whole project or process. It is easier to construct and use but normally does not yield as much feedback as an analytic rubric.

Sample Holistic Rubric

Score	Description	Self-assessment	Teacher assessment
1	All parts are included; demonstrates a clear and complete understanding.		
2	Key parts are included; demonstrates understanding		
3	Some key parts are missing; demonstrates partial understanding.		
4	Many key parts are missing; does not demonstrate understanding.		
5	Did not attempt project.		

GUIDELINES FOR ANALYTIC RUBRIC DESIGN

The analytic rubric requires that process or product be broken into discrete steps or parts to evaluate the extent to which the criteria are met. Analytic rubrics are helpful in allowing teachers and students to distinguish between a superior and inferior product or process.

Analytic rubrics include the clearly defined and stated important steps of the product or process, preferably in order of occurrence. They can be time consuming but provide excellent feedback, especially when students are involved in the construction and evaluation process.

Criteria	Beginning	Progressing	Proficient	Superior	Student assessment	Teacher assessment
1st Step Precise description of one important aspect of performance or product.	Description of fundamental level.	Description showing movement toward proficiency.	Description showing proficiency in performance.	Description showing superlative performance.		
2nd Step Precise description of another important aspect of performance or product.	Description of fundamental level.	Description showing movement toward proficiency.	Description showing proficiency in performance.	Description showing superlative performance.		
3rd Step Precise description of another important aspect of performance or product.	Description of fundamental level.	Description showing movement toward proficiency.	Description showing proficiency in performance.	Description showing superlative performance.		
4th Step Precise description of another important aspect of performance or product.	Description of fundamental level.	Description showing movement toward proficiency.	Description showing proficiency in performance.	Description showing superlative performance.		

(Adapted from Mertler, 2001; Stride, 2004)

Resources

Chapter 1

Boundy, Kathleen. 1992. *Promoting inclusion for all students with disabilities*. Cambridge, MA: Center for Law and Education.

ERIC Review. 1996. *Inclusion* 4, no. 3: i–37.

IDEA '97. The Individuals with Disabilities Education Act. Amendments of 1997. www.ed.gov/OSERS/policy/IDEA/

Lombardi, Thomas P., ed. 1999. *Inclusion: Policy and practice*. Bloomington, IN: Phi Delta Kappa Educational Foundation.

Salend S., J. Duhaney, and M. G. Laurel. 1999. The impact of inclusion on students with and without disabilities and their educators. *Remedial and Special Education* 20, no. 2 : 114–26.

Stride, June. 2004. *Practical strategies for including high school students with behavioral disabilities*. Verona, WI: IEP Resources.

US Department of Education: Office of Special Education and Rehabilitative Services. 2001. 22nd Annual Report to Congress on the Implementation of the Individuals with Disabilities Education Act.

Viadero, Debra. 2004. "What Works" Research site unveiled. *Education Week* 23, no. 42: 1, 33.

Yell, M. L., and A. Katsiyannis. 2000. Functional behavioral assessment and IDEA '97: Legal and practice considerations. *Preventing School Failure* 44: 158–162.

Yell, M. L., M. E. Rozalski and E. Drasgow. 2001. Disciplining students with disabilities. *Focus on Exceptional Children* 33, no. 9, 1–20.

Zigmond, Naomi. 2001. Special education at a crossroads. *Preventing School Failure* 45, no. 2: 70–75.

Zirkel, Perry A. 2001. Manifest determination. *Phi Delta Kappan* 82, no. 6: 478–79.

Websites

Association for Supervision and Curriculum Development
http://www.ascd.org/portal/site/ascd/index.jsp/

Circle of Inclusion
http://www.circleofinclusion.org/

Education Resources Information Center (ERIC)
http://www.eric.ed.gov/

National Institute for Urban School Improvement
http://www.urbanschools.org/

The Nation's Report Card
http://nces.ed.gov/nationsreportcard/

New Horizons for Learning
http://www.newhorizons.org/

Wrightslaw
Special education law and advocacy
http://www.wrightslaw.com/

Chapter 2

Cook, L., and M. Friend. 1995. What are some ways regular and special educators can work together effectively? *Focus on Exceptional Children* 28, no. 3.

Dieker, Lisa. *Co-teaching lesson plan book.* Council for Exceptional Children. [Available at www.cec.sped.org]

Driver, Barbara L. 1996. Where do we go from here? Sustaining and maintaining co-teaching relationships. *LD Forum* 21, no. 4: 29–32.

Mahoney, Michael. 1997. Small victories in an inclusive classroom. *Educational Leadership* 54, no. 7: 59–62.

Morefield, John. 1998. *Restructuring education: Recreating schools for all children.* Seattle, WA: New Horizons for Learning.

Ripley, Suzanne. 1997. Collaboration between general and special education teachers. Washington, DC: ERIC ED 409317.

Schmidt, Rauel J., Mary S. Rozendal, and Gretchen G. Greenman. 2002. Reading instruction in the inclusion classroom: Research-based practices. *Remedial and Special Education* 23, no. 3: 130–40.

Stride, June. 2004. *Practical strategies for including high school students with behavioral disabilities.* Verona, WI: IEP Resources.

Websites

Education Resources Information Center (ERIC)
ERIC is a national information system funded by the US Department of Education's Institute of Education Sciences to provide access to education literature.
http://www.eric.ed.gov/

Florida Inclusion Network
Ideas and resources to show how inclusion has worked in Florida.
http://www.floridainclusionnetwork.com

National Dissemination Center for Children with Disabilities (NICHCY).
A free federally funded information clearinghouse on special education services and resources.
(Call 1-800-695-0285 for help locating information)
http://www.nichcy.org/index.html

Wrightslaw
A fine site for locating up-to-date information about special education and the law. Many resources to help answer questions you may have.
http://www.wrightslaw.com

Chapter 3

Christenson, S. L., T. Rounds, and M. J. Franklin. 1992. Home-school collaboration: Effects, issues and opportunities. In *Home-school collaboration: Enhancing children's academic and social competence,* edited by S. L. Christenson and J. C. Conoley. Bethesda, MD: National Association of School Psychologists.

Inger, Morton. 1992. *Increasing the school involvement of Hispanic parents.* New York: Columbia University. ERIC ED 350380.

Ngeow, K. Y. 1999. Online resources for parent/family involvement. *ERIC Digest.* ERIC, ED 432775.

Parent involvement in education: A resource for parents, educators, and communities. 1998. Des Moines, IA: Iowa State Dept. of Education. ERIC, ED 387245.

Rules for working with parents. 1996. *The Master Teacher* 28, no. 25: 6. Leadership Lane, PO Box 1207, Manhattan, KS 66505-1207. Phone 1-800-699-9633.

Schwartz, W. 1999. School support for foster families. *ERIC/CUE Digest* 147. ERIC Clearinghouse on Urban Education. Teachers College, Columbia University, NY. Phone 800-601-4868.

Stride, June. 2004. *Practical strategies for including high school students with behavioral disabilities.* Verona, WI: IEP Resources.

US Department of Education. 2002. *Helping your child succeed in school.* Available in English or Spanish. Phone 1-877-4ED-PUBS or download from www.ed.gov/pubs/ [Search *parent input*]

US Department of Education. 1995. *Helping your child with homework.* Request Consumer Information Catalogue (free) from the Consumer Information Center, Pueblo, CO 81009.

US Department of Education. 2004. *No Child Left Behind: A toolkit for teachers.* Phone 1-877-433-7827 or email your request to edpubs@inet.ed.gov

Websites

The Children's Partnership
http://www.childrenspartnership.org/bbar/ctech.html

Dealing With Tough Issues Series: QuickTips® for Parents
http://www.parent-institute.com

Family Involvement in Children's Education:
Successful Local Approaches
http://www.ed.gov/pubs/ [Search *family involvement*]

Family TLC
Family parenting tips, activities, articles on child development.
http://familyTLC.net

Helping Your Child With Homework
http://www.ed.gov/pubs/ [Search *homework help*]

Kids Can Learn!
http://www.kidscanlearn.com/

The National Parent Information Network
http://www.npin.org/

North Central Regional Educational Laboratory
Parent Involvement: Literature Review and Database
of Promising Practices
http://www.ncrel.org/sdrs/pidata/pi0over.htm

Parenting TIPS: Timely Intervention Parental Strategies
http://www.drjunestride.com

Parents Guide to the Internet
http://www.ed.gov/pubs/parents/internet/index.html

TEAMS Educational Resources
http://teams.lacoe.edu/

SafeKids.Com
Child Safety on the Information Highway
http://www.safekids.com/child_safety.htm

Chapter 5

Ailes, R. 1995. *You are the message*. New York: Doubleday.

Covey, S. 1989. *The seven habits of highly effective people*. New York: Fireside.

French, N. 2000. Taking time to save time: Delegating to paraeducators. *Teaching Exceptional Children* 32, no. 3: 79–83.

IDEA '97. The Individuals with Disabilities Education Act. Amendments of 1997. www.ed.gov/OSERS/policy/IDEA/

Keller, B. 2003. Spotlight shining on over-looked paraeducators. *Education Week* 23, no. 40: 10–11.

Managing paraprofessionals in the classroom. 1997. *The Master Teacher* 28, no. 23: 1–6.

National Joint Committee on Learning Disabilities. 1999. Learning disabilities: Use of paraprofessionals. *Learning Disability Quarterly* 22, no. 1: 23–30.

Pickett, A. 1999. *Strengthening and supporting teacher/provider-paraeducator teams: Guidelines for paraeducator roles, supervision and preparation.* Washington, DC. Office of Special Education and Rehabilitative Services, Division of Personnel Preparation.

Pickett, A., K. Faison, and J. Formanek. 1999. *A core curriculum and training program to prepare paraeducators to work in inclusive classrooms serving school age students with disabilities.* 2d ed. New York: City University of New York, National Resource Center for Paraprofessionals in Education and Related Services.

US Department of Education. 2004. *The Achiever* 3, no. 12: 1–6.

Voltz, D. L., N. Brazil, and Alison Ford. 2001. What matters most in inclusive education: A practical guide for moving forward. *Intervention in School and Clinic* 37, no. 1: 23–30.

Warger, Cynthia. 2002–03. *Supporting paraeducators: A summary of current practices.* Arlington, VA. ERIC/OSEP Digest, Digest N E642.

Websites

Council for Exceptional Children
Answers questions about IDEA and supports your efforts to help all children learn.
http://www.ideapractices.org/

Council for Exceptional Children
Information Center on Disabilities and Gifted Education
http://www.ericec.org/

Gateway to 21st Century Skills
http://www.search.thegateway.org [Search *paraeducator*]

National Clearinghouse for Paraeducator Resources
http://www.usc.edu/dept/education/CMMR/Clearinghouse.html

Wrightslaw
http://www.wrightslaw.com/

Chapter 6

Clawson, D. 2003. *Strategies for winning over the impossible class.* Seattle, WA: New Horizons for Learning.

Dwyer, K. P. 1997. Disciplining students with disabilities. *National Association of School Psychologists Communique* 26: 2.

National Center for Injury Prevention and Control. 1999. *Best practices for preventing violence of children and youth: A sourcebook.* Atlanta, GA: Centers for Disease Control and Prevention.

NICHCY. 1999. *Interventions for chronic behavior problems* (Research Brief 1). Washington, DC: National Information Center for Children and Youth with Disabilities.

Van Acker, R. 1993. Dealing with conflict and aggression in the classroom: What skills do teachers need? *Teacher Education and Special Education* 16: 23–33.

Voltz, D., N. Brazil, and Alison Ford. 2001. What matters most in inclusive education: A practical guide for moving forward. *Intervention in School and Clinic* 37, no. 1: 23–30.

Workman, E. A., and M. M. Katz. 1995. *Teaching behavioral self-control to students.* 2d ed. Austin, TX: Pro Ed.

Websites

Center for Effective Collaboration and Practice
Fine resources prepared by the Chesapeake Institute for the US Department of Education Office of Special Education and Rehabilitation Services Offices of Special Education Programs.
http://cecp.air.org/resources/

New Horizons for Learning
Website devoted to teaching and learning strategies and special needs students.
http://www.newhorizons.org

NICHCY
Offers free resources for educating children and youth with behavioral disorders, including the Council for Exceptional Children's Mini-Library.
http://www.nichcy.org/

You Can Handle Them All
A superb free resource for the teacher eager to develop a repertoire of tried and true responses to difficult behaviors.
http://www.disciplinehelp.com/

Chapter 7

Algozzine B., and J. E. Ysseldyke. 1997. Time savers for educators. Paper presented at the Inclusion Conference, Uniondale, NY, April 24, 1998, 109–111.

Beckman, Pat. 2002. *Strategy instruction.* Arlington, VA. ERIC ED 474302.

Bohn, C., A. Roehrig, and M. Pressley. 2004. The first days of school of two more effective and four less effective primary-grades teachers. *The Elementary School Journal* 104, no. 1: 269–88.

Boone, M. and L. Avila. 1992. Wasn't that a good special education lesson? *NASSP Bulletin,* 89–94.

Burke, M. D., S. L. Hagan, and B. Grossen. 1998. What curricular designs and strategies accommodate diverse learners? *Teaching Exceptional Children* 31, no. 1: 34–38.

Federico, M. A., W. G. Hen-old, and J. Venn. 1999. Helpful tips for successful inclusion: A checklist for educators. *Teaching Exceptional Children* 32, no. 1: 76–82.

Johnston, R. 2004. Paper trail. *Teacher Magazine.* [Available at http://www.edweek.org/ew/articles/20004/06/23/41/flat_stanley]

Larkin, M. 2002. *Using scaffolded instruction to optimize learning.* Arlington, VA. ERIC ED 474301.

The Master Teacher Series. 1996–97. Vol. 28: nos. 1, 4, 5, 13. Leadership Lane, PO Box 1207, Manhattan, KS 66505, phone 1-800-669-9633.

Mastropieri, M. A., and T. E. Scruggs. 2000. *The inclusive classroom: Strategies for effective instruction.* Upper Saddle River, NJ: Prentice Hall.

Stride, J. 2004. *Practical strategies for including high school students with behavioral disabilities.* Verona, WI: IEP Resources.

Tomlinson, C. A. 1999. *The differentiated classroom: Responding to the needs of all learners.* Alexandria, VA: Association for Supervision and Curriculum Development.

Zemmelman, S., H. Daniels, and A. Hyde. 1993. *Best practice: New Standards for teaching and learning in America's schools.* Portsmouth, NH: Heinemann.

Websites

The Association for Supervision and Curriculum Development (ASCD)

Discusses differentiated instruction.
http://ascd.org/ (Education Topics)

Free online teachers workshops.
http://www.ed.gov/ (Teachers: Teacher-to-Teacher Initiative)

Washington State website about successful strategies and practices related to inclusion. Information can be freely copied as it is within the public domain.
http://www.newhorizons.org/ (Teaching and Learning Strategies)

Wrightslaw
Addresses the concept and expectation of research based instruction.
http://www.wrightslaw.com/nclb/4defs.reading.htm

Chapter 8

Bradley, D. 1998. Grading modified assignments: Equity or compromise. *Teaching Exceptional Children* 31, no. 2: 24–29.

Brualdi, A. 1998. Implementing performance assessment in the classroom. *Practical Assessment, Research and Evaluation* 6, no. 2: 1–5. [Available at www.ascd.org]

Byrnes, M. 2004. Alternate assessment FAQs (and answers). *Teaching Exceptional Children* 36, no. 6: 59–63.

Calkins, L., K. Montgomery, and D. Santman. 1999. *Helping children master the tricks and avoid the traps of standardized tests: A teacher's guide to standardized reading tests.* Portsmouth, NH: Heinemann.

Christensen, J. 1998. A decision for grading students. *Teaching Exceptional Children.* 31, no. 2: 30–35.

Heubert, J. P. 2002. *High-stakes testing: Opportunities and risks for students of color, English-language learners and students with disabilities.* Baltimore, MD: Johns Hopkins University Press.

Klingner, J., and S. Vaughn. 1999. Students' perceptions of instruction in inclusion classrooms: Implications for students with learning disabilities. *Exceptional Children* 66, no. 1: 23–37.

Linn, R. L. 2000. Assessments and accountability. *Educational Researcher* 29, no. 2: 4–16.

Mertler, C. A. 2001. Designing scoring rubrics for your classroom. *Practical Assessment, Research and Evaluation* 7, no. 25: 1–10.

Olson, L. 2005. ETS to enter formative-assessment market at K–12 level. *Education Week.* [Available at www.edweek.org/ew/ news/teaching-and-learning/]

Olson, L. 2004. "Value added" models gain in popularity. *Education Week.* [Available at www.edweek.org/ew/news/ teaching-and-learning/]

Stride, J. 2004. *Practical strategies for including high school students with behavioral disabilities.* Verona, WI: IEP Resources.

Tienken, C., and M. Wilson. 2001. Using state standards and tests to improve instruction. *Practical Assessment. Research and Evaluation* 7, no. 13: 1–8.

US Department of Education. 2002. Tests: Myths and realities. *Testing for results: Helping families, schools and communities understand and improve student achievement.* [Available at www.ed.gov/]